CHARACTER EDUCATION BOOK OF PLAYS

Elementary Level

by Judy Truesdell Mecca

Incentive Publications, Inc.
Nashville, Tennessee

Illustrated by Gayle Harvey
Cover by Becky Rüegger
Edited by Jean K. Signor

ISBN 978-0-86530-485-7

4   5   6   7   8   9   10   11   10   09   08

PRINTED IN THE UNITED STATES OF AMERICA
www.incentivepublications.com

Table of Contents

HONESTY

RESPONSIBILITY

COMMITMENT

COURAGE

Overview
Character Education Book of Plays
Elementary Level

It is a different world than when we, parents and educators, were growing up! Things we took for granted, such as keeping our word, living up to our obligations, and respecting our elders, seem to have become secondary to instant gratification, ego fulfillment, and money, money, money.

It is not too late to reverse this trend! Education can help reinvent the morals of this country, starting with our most valuable resource—our children. We should start now while the children are still young enough to be open to these profound ideas. There are many ways to teach lessons; certainly theatre arts is one of the best.

By incorporating acting, music, visual arts, communication skills and, most importantly, FUN, this collection of elementary-age appropriate plays, *Character Education Book of Plays — Elementary Level,* offers a tool in the quest for morality. Here are seven plays, dealing with values such as respect, honesty, responsibility, commitment, love, and courage. Each play is short enough to be presented during the school day, and most have accompanying teaching materials, such as class discussion topics and vocabulary worksheets. Every effort has been made to tell the teacher/director how to create costumes, properties, and scenery using items already found at school or items that can easily be found at home. Most of the plays have flexible casts; the chorus or other group parts can be as small or as large as each class requires.

These plays are not only classroom-friendly, but will be great for church groups, scouts, recreation centers, and camp. Put the play on for the rest of the grade, or have a community night and invite families and friends. Hand in hand—we can make a difference!

* Respect * Honesty * Responsibility * Commitment * love * courage * * * ** *

You Don't Love Me!
A Play About
Different Ways of Showing Love

Character Education Book of Plays
Elementary Level

You Don't Love Me!

CAST

Dad

Mom

Marcie Phillips

Matt Phillips, *Marcie's brother*

Mrs. Greenlee, *Marcie's teacher*

Class members, including:

    Sarah

    Bobby

    Annie

    Timmy

The rest of Marcie's class (chorus)

You Don't Love Me!

Notes to the Teacher/Director

"You don't love me, or you'd let me . . . stay up late . . . skip my bath . . . eat fast food . . . skip my homework." How many times have parents (and teachers) heard these accusations? Surely they KNOW we are showing our love for them by enforcing the rules; yet, it appears they need reminding now and then.

You Don't Love Me! is a play in which Marcie Phillips is convinced that no one loves her. Her teacher does not love her or any student because she requires that they turn in their homework or they must face the consequences of a zero in her gradebook. Her mother and father do not love her, because of the vegetables they make her eat and the fact that they want to help her remember to do her homework. Matt, her younger brother, would stop relentlessly teasing and tormenting Marcie if he really cared about her!

Character Education Book of Plays
Elementary Level

You Don't Love Me!

Marcie dozes over her book and has a dream in which the world turns upside down. Her teacher throws the students' work in the trash and says she does not care what they do until the bell rings. Mom does not cook dinner, suggesting that the kids eat ice cream and left-over Christmas candy. Matt does not even look up from his electronic game long enough to give her any grief at all. Instead of being overjoyed at these odd events, Marcie is completely bewildered! Doesn't her mother care about her enough to cook dinner? Doesn't Dad want to make sure she goes to bed on time? Marcie thought they loved her!

Marcie wakes up and realizes how foolish she has been. Through her dream, Marcie understands how these rules and regulations are really just the ways in which adults in her life care for her and show their love.

Properties, Scenery, Costumes

This play can be easily produced in the classroom. The scenic needs are minimal; one scene takes place in a classroom. Costumes are typically regular school clothes; props can be gathered easily or disregarded in favor of pantomime.

There are several places in which the play can be updated or personalized for your group:

- First, the teacher's name can be the teacher in your classroom, or another teacher in school.

- When Marcie mentions playing a game with Matt the night before which prevents her from completing her homework, feel free to use any game that is popular with your group.

- For Marcie's book, you may include your class's favorite book.

- Mom suggests that Matt eat some of the "candy from his Christmas stocking." Depending on the time of year, she may suggest Easter candy, or perhaps Halloween candy. Also, when Matt asks permission to visit his friend Brad, his mother says "Be back by . . . winter!" This is another line in the play that should be tailored to the the time of year. If you are producing the play in the fall, Mom could say that Matt needs to return by summer.

You Don't Love Me! ⊘♥

Properties

If you choose to use actual items for properties, or "props," they are listed below. Instead, you may wish to have your cast simply pantomime them. (Consider the dinner scene when making your decision. Should you gather plates, silverware, glasses, etc., or would pretending work as well for your group?) Of course, using real props gives a more interesting picture to your audience and your students may enjoy gathering them. The choice is yours.

- Plates, silverware, serving dishes, etc., for Phillips' family dinner
- A copy of a popular novel for Marcie
- A stack of notebooks and stapled papers to represent Class Members' China reports
- Mrs. Greenlee's purse, containing a can of soda and a magazine
- Dad's crossword puzzle and pencil
- Mom's nail file
- Matt's game—a hand-held electronic game, or the controls of a popular video game
- Matt's math book and pencil
- Mom's dishrag or sponge, for wiping off the table

Scenery

The play takes place in three basic areas: the Phillips' dining room, Marcie's bedroom, and Marcie's classroom. When the play begins, Marcie's bedroom and the dining room should already be in place. For her bedroom, you can push two or three chairs or desks together and cover them with a bedspread and pillows. A long flat table would work well if you have one in your classroom. Some stuffed animals, a school bag, and a bathrobe would add to the atmosphere of Marcie's room. This set is not moved or changed during the play.

You Don't Love Me!

The dining room table can also be made of desks pushed together and covered with a table cloth. An art table, lunchroom table, or a card table from a student's home would make a great dining room table. Then you will need to place free-standing chairs around the table; it is important to arrange them so that no actor's back is facing the audience.

The classroom will be quite simple; just arrange a desk for each student in the classroom scene. You will need a teacher's desk for Mrs. Greenlee. Be sure to provide a trash can next to Mrs. Greenlee's desk for the ill-fated China reports.

Costumes

Marcie, Matt, and the other Class Members should wear regular school clothes. You should probably age your actor portraying the role of Dad by dressing him in a tie or suit jacket. You may wish to dust his hair at the temples with baby powder. Likewise, you will want to age Mom just a bit; she may wear a skirt or pant suit or an apron. Mrs. Greenlee should find her best teacher outfit—skirt and blouse, dress, or cardigan sweater. She might even need a pair of glasses attached to a chain around her neck and a baby powder dusting as well.

You Don't Love Me! ⊘♥

Teaching Materials to Accompany *You Don't Love Me!*

Class Discussion

Discuss the different ways characters in the play show love towards Marcie.

- How did Mom show her love for Marcie?
- How about Dad?
- Do you think Matt really loves his sister?
- Would he be showing love for her more if he did not tease her?
- Do teachers love their students?
- Is that love shown by Mrs. Greenlee when she rewards good work with good grades and insists that the students turn in their homework?
- When Mrs. Greenlee gives Marcie a zero for failing to hand in her homework paper, is she demonstrating how much she cares for Marcie?
  Why or why not?

What are some other ways in which people express love?

- How do friends express love?
- Ask someone to share how his or her best friend has shown that he or she loves him.
- How is love for a pet demonstrated?
- Do you express love for your grandparents the same way you do to your parents? Why or why not?

Writing Exercise

While Marcie speaks her monologue, the teacher and other class members should set up the classroom scene. Depending upon how many boys and girls are in your classroom scene, you may need more time. Have your class experiment with adding lines to Marcie's monologue. What else might Marcie say? How would she be feeling? Choose the best lines and add them to the monologue if you need the extra time.

Vocabulary Worksheet

You Don't Love Me!

Matching

Match the word with the definition which is most correct.

1. _____ monologue   a. Moves toward in a threatening way

2. _____ increasingly   b. A speech given by one actor

3. _____ baffled   c. Confused, bewildered

4. _____ advances   d. Becoming more and more

5. _____ outburst   e. A loud, startling noise or remark

Multiple Choice

Pick the sentence in which the word in bold type is used most correctly.

6. _____ a. Grandma shook her cane **menacingly** at the boys who trampled her flowers.

   _____ b. The movie was **menacingly**; we could not sleep the night we saw it.

   _____ c. Mom and Dad talked so **menacingly** I could hardly hear them!

7. _____ a. His **muttering** car made quite a noise as it went down the street.

   _____ b. She was **muttering** quietly to herself as she tried to decide what to do.

   _____ c. Mom is always **muttering** me—I wish she would let me grow up!

8. _____ a. "This is a terrible **situation**," my father said when he saw our flat tire.

   _____ b. The room was so crowded, there was no place to **situation**.

   _____ c. I packed all my clothes for summer camp in my new **situation**.

9. Describe what is meant by **interrupting**. _____

_____

_____

10. "The teacher asked us if we knocked over the glue, but we were all **innocent**."

   Did the students knock the glue over?_____

You Don't Love Me!

A Play About
Different Ways of Showing Love

(It is dinnertime at the PHILLIPS' house; as the play begins, DAD is at the head of the table, MOM is bringing in the last of the meal, MARCIE and MATT are sitting at the table. MATT is happy and hungry and cannot wait to start eating. MARCIE has her head in her hands; she looks upset.)

Marcie   What a rotten day I had in school! I am never going back!

Dad   Why, Marcie? What do you mean it was rotten?

Matt   They put a new mirror in the girls' restroom and she had to look at herself! *(MARCIE makes a fist in MATT'S direction.)* Just kidding, just kidding, sister dear!

Mom   *(taking her seat)* Marcie, what on earth went wrong? Did someone hurt your feelings? Tell us all about it.

Marcie   It's my mean old teacher, Mrs. Greenlee *(or insert name of classroom teacher here)*. We had homework last night . . . which I forgot to do because I was playing Matt's new game *(or current fun after-school activity)* with Matt!

Matt   How nice of your little brother to share his games with you, Marcie! You must love him a lot!

Marcie   *(pretending to ignore him)* ANYWAY . . . so Mrs. Greenlee told us to turn the homework in and I didn't have it, and she gave me a "zero" in her gradebook!

Dad   Marcie, I am very disappointed to hear that you had homework last night and you did not do it!

You Don't Love Me!

Mom	So am I, Marcie! Is there any way that we can help you remember when you have homework? We do not want this to happen again.
Matt	I think the answer is—new brain for Marcie!
Dad	Matt, let's see if we can help your big sister.
Marcie	You're giving Matt away! Thanks so much! That WILL help me!
Mom	I have an idea. I'll put a little notepad up on the refrigerator, and every day you can come in and write your homework assignments on it! That way, I'll be able to help you remember!
Marcie	*(Muttering under her breath)* You mean you will gripe at me . . .
Mom	What's that, dear?
Marcie	Nothing, Mom. That probably will be good.

(They eat in silence for a moment, then:)

Marcie	*(In a loud voice)* But that's not all that went wrong!

(The family jumps, startled by MARCIE'S outburst.)

Dad	What else?
Marcie	At recess, some boys were picking on my best friend Sarah, and I went over and told them to leave her alone and Mrs. Greenlee made us all go sit on a bench for the rest of the time!
Mom	Poor Mrs. Greenlee. It must be hard to know whom to punish in a situation like that.
Marcie	Poor Mrs. Greenlee? Poor Mrs. Greenlee?! I don't feel sorry for her. I think she hates kids, that's what I think.
Matt	She really used to like kids until she had you in her class.

You Don't Love Me!

Dad Matt . . .

Matt Don't mind me, I'm just eating.

(They eat for a moment, in silence, then MARCIE says:)

Marcie And that's not all!

(Again the family jumps, startled.)

Mom What else, Marcie?

Marcie She did not give us any free time in class to read or to draw or to do anything fun. It was just work, work, work right up until the bell rang to go home.

Dad I know what you mean! At my job, some days seem to go on forever!

Mom I'm sorry you had a bad day, dear. Maybe tomorrow will be better. Now eat your peas.

Marcie I hate peas! Why do you make things for supper that I can't stand!

Mom Marcie, you have to eat vegetables! Your bones need them, and your eyes . . .

Matt But if she couldn't see, she wouldn't have to look at herself in the mirror anymore! That could be a good thing!

Marcie *(Getting up from the table)* That's it! I'm not hungry . . . for peas or anything else! I'm going to my room to read my book! *(or insert current popular book here.)*.

Dad Marcie, wait. I hate to ask you this, but do you have homework tonight?

Marcie No, I do not. As if any of you care! No one loves me!

(She exits.)

❤ You Don't Love Me!

Matt   All right! More food for me! Pass the chicken, please!

Mom & Dad   Matt . . .

(MOM, DAD & MATT clear away the table and dinner things from center stage, then exit. CLASS MEMBERS set up the classroom, then quietly take their places in the classroom and "freeze." MARCIE is in her bedroom, stage right, sitting on her bed or in a chair, with her favorite book.)

Marcie   Nobody loves me! Mrs. Greenlee makes me do my work and won't let me play at recess . . . Mom and Dad want me to do my homework . . . and eat my peas! And Matt . . . Matt is such an annoying little creep . . . why I ought to . . . I ought to . . . *(she closes her eyes and drops her book)*

(The CLASS MEMBERS "come to life," and begin to talk among themselves. MRS. GREENLEE speaks to the class.)

Mrs. Greenlee   All right, class, pipe down. *(Looking around)* Where's Marcie? Marcie Phillips! Yoo hoo!

(Hearing her name, MARCIE opens her eyes.)

Marcie   What? Where am I? Oh! I must be late for school! *(She hurries over to the classroom set and takes her seat.)*

Mrs. Greenlee   So glad you could join us, Marcie.

Sarah   *(Whispering to MARCIE)* I hope you remembered your homework this time!

Marcie   My homework? Uh . . .

Mrs. Greenlee   Boys and girls, let me have your attention please. We are finished with our unit on the customs of China. I have all of your reports. Thank you for your hard work. I've read them all . . . and here's a surprise for you! *(She takes the stack of notebooks, stapled papers, etc. and drops them into the trash can.)* I'm really sick of reading this stuff! I want to

You Don't Love Me!

read a good mystery novel for a change! So there—I hope you learned something!

(The class is quiet for a moment, then:)

Patty   Are you taking a grade?

Mrs. Greenlee   Nope.

Bobby   What about the spelling test?

Mrs. Greenlee   What spelling test?

Bobby   We have a spelling test every Friday!

Mrs. Greenlee   Oh yeah. I guess I forgot.

Annie   You forgot our spelling test? This can't be happening!

Mrs. Greenlee   You boys and girls can do whatever you want from now until the bell rings. I will be drinking this soda and reading a magazine!

(She takes a can of soda out of her purse and pops the top. Then she pulls out a magazine and begins to read it. The class sits for a minute, looking at each other. They are shocked. TIMMY jumps up.)

Timmy   Can we go outside?

Mrs. Greenlee   Do whatever you want, I don't care!

(The class exits, cheering, excited to be headed for another recess. MARCIE walks to the front of the acting area and has a brief monologue. While she talks, the CLASS MEMBERS and MRS. GREENLEE strike the school scenery and re-set the PHILLIPS' dining room, with one chair away from the table for MATT. MOM and DAD sit at the table, and MATT sits in the chair that is away from the table. They freeze during MARCIE'S speech.)

Marcie   *(Toward the audience)* What is going on? This is the weirdest thing that's ever happened! Mrs. Greenlee throwing our reports in the trash?! Not taking a grade?! Forgetting our spelling test?! That's never happened in the history of school! And saying she

Character Education Book of Plays
Elementary Level

⊘♥ You Don't Love Me!

doesn't care if we go outside! But here's the weirdest thing . . . I know I SHOULD be happy! I mean, if she doesn't care what we do—then I'm out of the homework business for good! But it just feels . . . wrong! Oh, well. I'll go home. I can always count on good old Mom and Dad to remember all the rules and pester me about them . . .

(MARCIE enters the PHILLIPS' dining room area. She is shocked to see DAD working a crossword puzzle at the table, MOM filing her nails, and MATT sitting away from the table, playing a game.)

Marcie	Mom? Dad?
Mom	Oh, hi, Marcie. How was school?
Marcie	It was really weird. Hi, Dad.
Dad	Hi, Marcie, what's a four-letter word that means "caring and fondness"?
Marcie	Love.
Dad	Right! That works! Thanks.
Matt	Hi, Marcie.
Marcie	Hi, Matt . . . what, no smart remark?
Matt	What? Oh, no, I guess not. *(to himself, about his game)* All right! He makes a touchdown!
Marcie	Mom—what's for dinner? I'm starved!
Mom	Oh, you know what? I didn't really make any dinner. Matt had some potato chips and candy from his Christmas stocking *(or left over from Easter or Halloween)* . . . there's some soda in there, and I think some ice cream.
Marcie	*(sitting down at the table)* I don't have to eat any meat or vegetables?

You Don't Love Me! 🚫❤️

Mom   Well, you probably should, but I just didn't feel like opening a can or fighting with you about it. You can eat whatever your little heart desires!

Marcie   I guess maybe I'm not so hungry after all . . .

Dad   Do you have any homework, Marcie?

Marcie   *(looking up, rather excited, thinking that DAD seems to be asking a normal question)* Um . . . no . . . I mean, I don't think I do . . . see, Mrs. Greenlee was acting really weird . . .

Dad   *(interrupting her)* That's nice. There's a good movie on television tonight—it lasts until after midnight. Want to watch it with us?

Marcie   Sure, I guess . . .

Mom   That's pretty late . . . but oh well, who cares? A good movie is worth being a little sleepy tomorrow, isn't that right, Marcie girl?

Marcie   I don't know . . .

Matt   Mom, can I go over to Brad's house?

Mom   Are his parents at home?

Matt   No.

Mom   Sure. Be back by . . . winter! *(or some other far-off season or holiday)*

Matt   Not a problem! *(He exits.)*

Dad   That crazy Matt. He told me he wants to stop throwing his paper route in the mornings! He says it's too hard to get up!

Mom   Really?

Dad   Yep. So I told him that was OK with me.

⊘ You Don't Love Me!

Mom Good for you! Maybe now he won't disturb us when he bumps around in the dark!

(MOM and DAD laugh together, while MARCIE becomes increasingly unsettled.)

Marcie Dad? Mom? Why are you acting this way? Don't you care about us? Don't you want us to eat good food and get enough sleep?

Dad Well, of course we care about you, Marcie. We love you!

Mom We love you enough to let you do whatever you want!

Marcie *(Now completely baffled)* I'll . . . I'll be in my room if you need me.

Dad Sounds fine, dear!

Mom While you're in there . . . oh, never mind!

Marcie What?

Mom I was about to ask you to clean up your room! How mean!

Marcie I've got to get outta here . . .

(She exits to her bedroom, and MOM and DAD freeze at the table. MARCIE flops on her bed.)

This is awful! No work at school—no dinner—no smart remarks from Matt! What's wrong with everybody? I thought they cared about my health and my school work . . . I thought they loved me . . . *(She seems to doze.)*

(MATT re-enters and joins his parents at the table. He has a school book open and DAD is helping him with some homework. MOM is wiping off the table. MARCIE sits up, rubs her eyes, and heads for the dining room.)

You Don't Love Me!

Mom	Hi, Marcie! Did you take a little nap?
Matt	She didn't take a nap—I don't see her itty witty blankie!
Marcie	What did you say, Matt?
Matt	*(pretending to be innocent)* Oh, nothing! I just thought I'd see your little snuggly blankie that you've slept with every night since you were an itty witty girl . . .
Marcie	*(perking up)* Are you teasing me? Are you trying to make me mad?
Dad	Matt, leave your sister alone and let's get back to this math homework. Now, let's do this problem again; it just does not look right to me. *(They go back to work.)*
Mom	Marcie, honey, are you feeling all right? You hardly ate any dinner and now you've fallen asleep. *(feels MARCIE'S forehead.)* Do you want me to make you some soup? I was about to slice up an apple; do you want a piece?
Marcie	Oh Mom, I had the weirdest dream! I mean, I guess it was a dream . . . but you were there . . . and you . . . and you . . .
Matt	And Toto, too!
Dad	Matt, let's stay on task here.
Matt	Sorry.
Marcie	Oh, it was awful! You didn't make dinner; you just let us eat whatever we wanted . . . and Mrs. Greenlee didn't give us any work and just read a magazine at her desk . . . and Matt didn't even tease me . . .

Character Education Book of Plays
Elementary Level

⊘♥ You Don't Love Me!

Matt   That WAS a dream!

Mom   Oh, Marcie, don't you see? I love you too much to be that kind of mother! I make good food for you because I do love you, not because I don't! And that's the reason I remind you to do your homework, and clean up your room and go to bed on time. Because I want to help make you healthy—and teach you good habits to last your whole life!

Dad   Of course, Marcie, that's why we have rules.

Marcie   I get it now. I've just been acting dumb.

Matt   Acting?

Mom   Marcie, I have a little secret for you. *(MOM puts her arm around MARCIE and "whispers" to her.)* Matt only teases you because he loves you! That's his way of showing it!

Matt   What, Mom? What did you say? Acch! Yuchh! Get me some of those fizzy little tablets! I think I'm gonna be sick!

Marcie   I get it, Mom, I get it. And here's how I show Matt how much I love him . . . *(She advances on MATT, menacingly, with her hands outstretched as though to strangle him, or a fist raised as though to pound him.)*

Matt   Uh . . . hey wait, Marcie . . . let's talk about this . . . wanta play a game? *(He exits, with MARCIE chasing him, and MOM and DAD laughing.)*

(As MARCIE and MATT run offstage, the rest of the cast joins MOM and DAD for the final song.)

You Don't Love Me!

Cast	WHAT IS LOVE? HOW DO YOU SHOW IT? SOMETIMES YOU SEE IT, BUT YOU JUST DON'T KNOW IT!
Mom & Dad	YOUR MOM AND DAD MAY PESTER YOU BUT THEY ONLY WANT WHAT'S BEST FOR YOU
Cast	CLEAN UP YOUR ROOM, EAT ALL YOUR PEAS LOVE IS SHOWN IN BOTH OF THESE
Mrs. Greenlee	"TURN IN YOUR HOMEWORK," TEACHERS SAY "AND YOU'LL BE IN (FIFTH)* GRADE SOMEDAY!" *(Insert next year's grade)
Girls in Cast	PESKY LITTLE BROTHERS MAKE US MAD
Boys in Cast	AW, YOU KNOW WE'RE NOT SO BAD . . .
Girls in Cast	YES YOU ARE, BUT WE GET THE PICTURE YOU SECRETLY WORSHIP YOUR BIG SISTER!

(Boys pantomime gagging and being sick)

Cast	SO LISTEN EVERYBODY, YOUNG AND OLD HERE'S SOME ADVICE; IT'S GOOD AS GOLD
	LOOK FOR LOVE AS YOU GO ABOUT YOUR DAY AND WE LOVE YOU FOR COMING TO OUR PLAY!

(Waving)

GOODBYE, EVERYBODY!

Character Education Book of Plays
Elementary Level

You Don't Love Me!

"All Kinds Of Love"

Lyrics by Judy Truesdell Mecca

Music by Jenifer Truesdell Christman

You Don't Love Me!

Here's some ad - vice; It's as good as gold. Look for love as you go a - bout your day and we love you for com - ing to our play!

Character Education Book of Plays
Elementary Level

THE BIG SWITCHEROO

A Play About
Respect

Character Education Book of Plays
Elementary Level

THE BIG SWITCHEROO

CAST

Respect Raccoon

Silver Fox

The Rabbit Family
  Granny Rabbit
  Grandpa Rabbit
  Mama Rabbit
  Hoppy
  Jumpy
  Springy
  Bouncy
  Skippy
  (Any others you
    would like to add)

The Squirrel Family
  Mom Squirrel
  Dad Squirrel
  Earl Squirrel

The Mouse Family
  Mommy Mouse
  Daddy Mouse
  Double Click

The Chipmunk Family
  Meemaw Chipmunk
  Pawpaw Chipmunk
  Alvin

THE BIG SWITCHEROO

Notes to the Teacher/Director

There's a little trouble brewing in The Big Hollow Tree. Four families share the tree: the Squirrels, the Rabbits, the Chipmunks, and the Mice. Lately, the young people seem to be a little short in their answers to their parents and grandparents. They respond to questions with words like "Huh?" and "Whatever." There seems to be a shortage of appreciation for the favors the older folks do for the younger ones; "thank you" is seldom heard. When the parents and grandparents need help carrying in heavy supplies for the winter, or repairing the trunk of the tree where woodpeckers have pecked holes, the young people do not seem to be able to stop playing long enough to help out. Something is missing . . .

Enter Respect Raccoon, the coolest raccoon in the forest. He swings in through the audience, shaking hands and patting folks on the back. He is joined by his sidekick Silver Fox, and the play begins to unfold. As "RR" and Silver Fox look on from the sidelines, we see several examples of the young people's lack of . . . something . . . for their elders. Finally, he freezes everyone and, saying a magic chant, turns young characters into old and old into young. The (formerly) young characters are dismayed! Just listen to that tone of voice! How selfish! How . . . disrespectful! When they finally realize that respect is the missing ingredient in the little community within the Big Hollow Tree, Respect Raccoon switches everyone back with yet another magic chant. Everyone hugs and all the children vow to treat their elders with the respect that they certainly deserve.

This is a light-hearted, slightly magical play in which a great deal of humor is incorporated into the dialogue, and many kids get a chance to speak. If you need to include more youngsters, add more Rabbits, and give them other fun names. If you do not have a group quite large enough to fill all the roles as written, simply remove a family and redistribute their lines.

THE BIG SWITCHEROO

It might be wise to make sure your cast understands some theatrical conventions used in this play. For instance, there are a few places in which characters are called upon to *ad-lib*. Make sure your class understands that this means to say lines which are consistent with their characters, and what their characters would say—but not written down in the script.

A *stage whisper* is also mentioned—make sure they realize that this is a line which is delivered in such a way that the actor seems to be whispering to the actor next to him (in this case Respect Raccoon and Silver Fox), yet the actor is speaking loudly enough for the audience to hear what is being said. The actor may wish to put a hand to the side of his mouth to help create this illusion.

Finally, *upstaging* should be discussed. Upstaging occurs when an actor who is not supposed to be the center of attention or focus at a particular moment in the play does something to attract attention to himself. In this play, Respect Raccoon and Silver Fox sit to the side of the stage for most of the play. Though they should be reacting in small, realistic ways to the action of the other characters, their movements should never be large and distracting, nor should they speak until they have scripted lines. This is not only helpful to the audience (who should be watching the other characters at that time), but it is considered common courtesy to the other members of the cast. In fact . . . it is a way of showing respect for one's fellow actors.

Some vocabulary words included in the play are listed below. If your class is not familiar with some of these words, you may wish to have them work the Vocabulary Worksheet individually, or as a class.

common

expressions

affection

coincidence

original

dread

amused

familiar

Have fun! Make bunny ears! Paint on whiskers! And remember . . . respect . . . rules!

THE BIG SWITCHEROO

Properties

As with some of the other plays, there are some choices you can make regarding properties. As it is written, Respect Raccoon and Silver Fox are the only ones who utilize real props. They need:

- A beach bag or other handled bag
- A cold drink (perhaps with curly straw)
- Popcorn in a bag or bowl
  (or previously popped in a microwave packet)
- Raisinets™
- A pine bough or other "magic wand" to wave over the cast

The rest of the properties are pantomimed; the play is written this way. If you and your cast would like, of course, you can gather the real things. Just remove Silver Fox's line, "Why is he pantomiming?" and Respect Raccoon's answer, "Low budget show. No money for props."

Here are the rest of the properties you'll need if you decide to go three-dimensional:

- Earl Squirrel's comic book or paperback
- The Rabbit Children's "Bunny" dolls. (Take traditional 12-inch fashion dolls and attach construction paper rabbit ears to their heads.)
- "Bunny" doll clothes, including a doctor's outfit
- A tray of cookies and small cartons of milk (not as likely to spill and the audience can't see whether they are actually empty or not)
- Heavy bags and boxes for the Mom characters to carry. If you like, they could have greens and berries showing from the tops.
- Buckets, brushes and other hole-repairing equipment for the Dad and Grandfather characters

Scenery

Not too much! Respect Raccoon and Silver Fox need chairs stage right. These can be regular classroom chairs, or you might want to round up a director's chair for Respect Raccoon.

It might be fun to draw the outline of The Hollow Tree on the chalkboard, or to use butcher paper to draw branches and hang them from the ceiling. You can do as little or as much as you like for the families' areas. Each area could have a little table and chairs, and perhaps some art on the table such as a class-created family portrait (see *Art Projects*). You could give each family a color—rabbits are white, chipmunks are brown, squirrels are red, mice are gray—and put a coordinating table cloth on the table in each. (This is really just for fun—most of the action takes place in the center stage common area and no scenery is needed there.)

Costumes

Your class/cast can be quite creative as you design costumes for these animals.

Respect Raccoon should wear something "cool" such as a Hawaiian shirt, jeans, and sandals or "flip-flops" if the weather is warm. Of course he needs a "mask"—you might experiment with a small black Halloween mask, but you'll probably have more luck drawing it on using theatrical make-up (from a theatrical supply or magic store) or black eyeliner. If you use make-up, be careful not to get too close to your actor's eyes—it can be quite painful and distracting! Paint the tip of his nose black and add some whiskers to his or her cheeks. You may wish to fashion a striped tail out of fake fur or other fabric and safety-pin it to the seat of his jeans.

Silver Fox should be dressed in . . . guess what? something silver! Maybe you can find a silver football jersey (the Dallas Cowboys, for instance) or

a silver shirt from a store that sells dance costumes. If you've cast Silver Fox as a girl, an entire silver outfit should be easier to locate. Do try to secure something silver rather than gray, since your Mouse characters will be gray. If you are just able to track down a silver top or shirt, black jeans or sweat pants should do fine for the rest of the costume. You might like to add some speedy athletic shoes, since he is so bouncy and active.

Fashion a pointy nose for Silver Fox out of construction paper and staple a slender piece of elastic to go around the back of the head like a mask. Enlist your creative cast to help decide what Silver Fox's tail should be made of—silver Christmas tinsel? White fake fur spray-painted lightly with silver? You may wish to choose something sturdier than construction paper since this character sits down for much of the play.

For the Squirrel Family, dress each one in red—sweats outfits, red sweatshirts and jeans, red T-shirts and jeans, etc. Female characters may wish to wear skirts. Then add costume pieces to indicate age: baseball caps and hair clips for the young generation, glasses and aprons for the older characters. Dust the hair of the older characters with baby powder. For noses and whiskers, make slightly pointed noses out of red or brown construction paper and staple elastic to them so that your actors wear them like a mask. Then affix brown pipe cleaners to the side for whiskers, or simply color in nose tips and draw whiskers on cheeks with brown eyeliner or other brown make-up. If you like, you can make tails out of fake fur or other fabric and attach it with a safety pin to the seats of all pants or skirts.

The same plan will work for the Mouse Family. Make their color gray and give them pink pipe cleaners and/or pink noses. If you go the make-up route rather than construction paper and elastic, you may wish to experiment with pink (blush) nose tips and gray drawn-on whiskers. Their tails are skinnier and longer than their bushy-tailed neighbors—use pink braided yarn or a roll of pink corduroy or other fabric pinned to their pants. Add age-indicating costume pieces and you are set.

Cast your "cleanest" students as the rabbits, because the Rabbit Family will wear all white. As with the other families, choose from white sweats outfits, t-shirts, etc.

Rabbit ears are definitely encouraged for these actors. Here are some suggestions: Cut ears out of stiff cardboard and glue them to plastic headbands. Or, cut white ears (perhaps with pink centers) out of double thickness of construction paper and bobby-pin them to your actors' heads.

Your rabbit noses and whiskers can be done with make-up, perhaps gray, or you might want to experiment with an "egg carton" nose. Cut an individual egg holder out of a cardboard egg carton. Staple elastic to the sides, and attach pink or gray pipe cleaner whiskers. Oh—and don't forget a white puff ball on the seat of the pants! Use cotton balls or cheerleader / drill team "shoe pom-pons"—little balls of fluff with jingle bells in the middle and shoe laces attached. Maybe the shoelaces could tie onto your actors' belts. Hint: Remove jingle bells or stuff cotton inside—so that the bells will not jingle whenever the Rabbits are on stage.

The Chipmunk Family can wear all brown. It would be fun to incorporate some black stripes; however, something to keep in mind is whether they all can find matching brown and black striped t-shirts or sweat shirts at a discount store. Or could black stripes of felt be cut and attached to plain brown tops?

Black whiskers are needed for the Chipmunk faces. As with the other families, the whiskers can be made of construction paper or egg cartons and pipe cleaners, or painted on with that ever-shortening black eye lining pencil. Tails can be made out of fake fur or other fabric and attached to pants or skirts.

THE BIG SWITCHEROO

Teaching Materials to Accompany *The Big Switcheroo*

Art Projects

Depending upon how elaborate you plan to be with your staging, you may wish to make some framed art prints to hang on the walls or stand on the tables in the individual animals' homes. Have your class choose a family and draw a family portrait. Have everyone vote on the best portrait per family, frame with construction paper, and use it as part of the set. (You may wish to use the others as the back side, or front cover, of programs! Have someone type the cast names on a computer, or write them out by hand.)

You can also have a day of making noses, whiskers and tails! See *Costumes.*

Class Discussion

1. See if your class can think of times when they were spoken to disrespectfully by another classmate, an employee in a store, a relative, etc.

    • How did they feel?

    • Was it worse when it was a grown-up or when it was one of their friends?

    • Was there ever a time when they spoke disrespectfully to someone else?

    • How could the same thing have been said in a respectful manner?

2. Discuss ways in which a high elected official, such as the president of the United States or the governor of a state, shows respect for the people who voted for him.

Character Education Book of Plays
Elementary Level

Vocabulary Worksheet

THE BIG SWITCHEROO

1. *Debbie, Kathy, Mike,* and *Steve* are names that were **common** when your parents were in school. What are some **common** names of boys and girls today?

   _____

   _____

2. What sort of **expression** would you be likely to see on the face of a little boy or girl on Christmas morning?

   _____

   _____

3. Which of these would you and your friends be most likely to **dread**?

   _____ a. A camping trip

   _____ b. Trick-or-treating on Halloween

   _____ c. Getting a shot at the doctor's office

4. If something is **familiar**, does it look strange and new? _____

Matching

Match the word with the definition which is most correct.

5. _____ original

6. _____ affection

7. _____ coincidence

8. _____ amused

a. Caused to smile or laugh

b. Feeling of fondness or love

c. One-of-a kind

d. Two things happening accidentally at the same time but seeming to have a connection

THE BIG SWITCHEROO

A Play About Respect

(The play begins when RESPECT RACCOON enters and walks through the audience. He is a very hip raccoon, wearing a Hawaiian shirt and carrying a shopping bag, possibly sipping on a cold drink. RR greets audience members, shakes hands with people, asks them how they're doing, are they in a good mood, etc., ad-libbing as he goes along. RR makes his way to the stage or acting area and faces the audience.)

Respect Raccoon   Hello, ladies and gentlemen, boys and girls, and welcome to our play, The Big Switcheroo. My name is Respect Raccoon— how do you do? *(He bows low, gracefully.)* Allow me to introduce my sidekick, Silver Fox.

(SILVER FOX enters, runs excitedly over to RESPECT RACCOON, and enthusiastically waves at the audience.)

Silver Fox   Hey, RR! Get it? RR? Respect Raccoon! I made that up myself! *(Giggles)* I'm SO EXCITED that I get to be in the play with you! I know how it turns out— *(to audience)* See, there were these kids, and they were acting . . .

Respect Raccoon   Whoa! Hold it there, dude! Don't give away the ending! We've got the whole play to show them the story!

Silver Fox   Sorry, RR. I get carried away.

Respect Raccoon   No worries, Silver. Well, let's get started, shall we?

Silver Fox   I'm ready!

Respect Raccoon   We live in the Forest of Good Feelings. This big hollow tree right here *(indicates the hollow tree portion of the set)* is called . . . I forget, what's it called?

Silver Fox   The Big Hollow Tree.

Respect Raccoon   Yeah, that's right. Anyway, there are four families who share The Big Hollow Tree, and here they are. This is the Squirrel Family *(Squirrel Family enters and faces the audience)*. This is Mom Squirrel and Dad Squirrel and Earl Squirrel, their son. *(The members of THE SQUIRREL FAMILY wave and take their place in the Squirrel area of the set, where they freeze.)*

Silver Fox   Can I introduce the next family?

Respect Raccoon Be my guest.

Silver Fox Coming to our stage right now is a family that needs no introduction. So, I won't introduce them. Just kidding! I crack myself up. Anyway, here is the Mouse Family! *(MOUSE FAMILY enters and faces the audience.)* There is Mommy Mouse and Daddy Mouse, and their little girl Double Click Mouse. *(They also wave and then take their places in the Mouse House, where they freeze.)* Double Click. That's a funny name for a mouse.

Respect Raccoon Now, here is the next family in the Big Hollow Tree—the Rabbits! Here are Granny and Grandpa Rabbit, *(GRANNY and GRANDPA RABBIT, elderly rabbits, enter)* Mama Rabbit . . .

Silver Fox Where's Papa Rabbit?

Respect Raccoon Something about a stew . . .

Silver Fox Oh, I wish you hadn't told me that!

Respect Raccoon And here are the kids . . . Flopsy, Mopsy *(Two little rabbits enter, but they stop and put their hands on their hips and look angry)*. Oh sorry, wrong story. These fine rabbits are Hoppy, Jumpy, Springy, Bouncy, and Skippy . . . *(As these rabbits are being named, each one bounces in and stands with MAMA RABBIT.)*

Silver Fox Not very original names!

Respect Raccoon Rabbit families are usually large—I'm sure they run out after a while.

(The whole RABBIT FAMILY looks annoyed, then crosses to the Rabbit area of the set, where they freeze.)

Silver Fox And last but not least—can I do this one too?

Respect Raccoon Certainly.

Silver Fox Last but not least—the Chipmunks! Meemaw Chipmunk, Pawpaw Chipmunk, and their grandson Alvin!

(THE CHIPMUNKS enter, wave to the audience, and take their places in their home, where they freeze.)

Silver Fox	Where are the parents? Never mind, I don't want to know.
Respect Raccoon	Don't worry—they're taking a little vacation. The kids are staying with the grandparents.
Silver Fox	Whew!

(During the next speech, the families come to life. The ADULTS and EARL SQUIRREL exit, and the rest of the boys and girls sit down and pantomime talking among themselves. SILVER FOX sets up two chairs far stage right for himself and RESPECT RACCOON.)

Respect Raccoon	Now, this is a great bunch of folks, and a great hollow tree. Besides their own rooms, they have a big common area where they can cook and hang out together, and the kids can play together—it's great. Except that lately . . . well, you can see for yourself. I love to watch this part.

(SILVER FOX has taken his seat and gotten popcorn out of RACCOON'S bag.)

Silver Fox	I got the popcorn!
Respect Raccoon	Raisinets?
Silver Fox	*(as he pulls them out of the bag)* Comin' up!
Respect Raccoon	*(as he takes his seat and takes some popcorn)* Watch this—and see if you can tell what's starting to go wrong in this hollow tree.

(EARL SQUIRREL enters, pantomiming holding a comic book or other paperback in his hand, and waving it around excitedly.)

Earl Squirrel	Hey! Hey guys! Alvin! Double Click! Hoppy! Look!
Silver Fox	*(In a stage whisper)* Why is he pantomiming?
Respect Raccoon	*(also stage-whispering)* Low budget show. No money for props.
Double Click Mouse	What is it, Earl? *(sees the book)* Wait? Is that what I think it is?
Earl Squirrel	It's the new People-morphs book!
Alvin Chipmunk	Cool, I've been wanting to read it! It's about these teenage animals who can morph into people!

THE BIG SWITCHEROO

Double Click Mouse Right! To protect the Forest of Good Feelings from aliens!

Hoppy As if people could save the forest from anything! What a goofy idea!

Earl Squirrel It's still a great book. Do you guys want to read it with me?

Double Click Mouse, Hoppy and Alvin Sure!

(DOUBLE CLICK, ALVIN, HOPPY and EARL SQUIRREL gather in one area and begin to read this book silently together. The RABBIT CHILDREN are playing in another part of the common area.)

Jumpy We'll read it later . . . right now we're too busy playing with our fashion dolls—Bunnies!

Springy I love Bunny. She's so cute and has so many great outfits! This is my favorite—Dr. Bunny!

Bouncy For my birthday, I've asked for her car . . .

Skippy I've asked for her Dream Hollow Tree!

Jumpy I know we'll get what we asked for for our birthday. We always do!

(GRANNY RABBIT and MEEMAW CHIPMUNK enter with pantomime cookies and milk. They go first to The RABBIT CHILDREN.)

Granny Rabbit Hello, you little wild hares! How about a snack?

Meemaw Chipmunk We baked them ourselves!

(The RABBIT CHILDREN snatch cookies and milk greedily and continue playing, without saying a word of thanks.)

Granny Rabbit Well, you kids must have been hungry! There isn't even a crumb left for the other children.

Bouncy What?

Meemaw Chipmunk She said that you kids must have . . .

Jumpy *(impatiently)* We heard. *(back to her sisters)* Let's dress Bunny up in her prom dress.

Springy Does she have a date?

THE BIG SWITCHEROO

Meemaw Chipmunk Come on, Granny Rabbit. Let's go make another batch, what do you say?

Granny Rabbit You know I love to bake! *(she crosses over to the CHILDREN who are reading together.)* Kids, Meemaw Chipmunk and I are about to bake some fresh acorn honey cookies and we'll bring you a bunch while they're still warm!

Alvin *(hardly looking up)* Huh?

Granny Rabbit I said we're going to make you some cookies. Would you like that?

Double Click Mouse Sure. Whatever.

Hoppy Yeah, I guess.

(GRANNY RABBIT and MEEMAW CHIPMUNK exit to the kitchen area. MOM SQUIRREL, MOMMY MOUSE and MAMA RABBIT enter pantomiming carrying big heavy bags. They are puffing and obviously struggling with the heavy load. When they arrive at center stage, they stop and put down their parcels.)

Mom Squirrel Ow! My aching back!

Mommy Mouse No kidding! This is quite a heavy load! But I'm so excited about all the things we were able to gather this morning!

Mama Rabbit We really had good luck. Acorns, blackberries, roots . . .

Mom Squirrel Chestnuts, mulberries—and a whole crabapple!

Mommy Mouse I don't know how you have managed to carry that whole crabapple all by yourself!

Mom Squirrel I'm Mighty Mom, that's how!

(The CHILDREN have stopped reading and playing and are looking at the MOTHERS, watching them carry in the food they have gathered.)

Mama Rabbit I'm not worried about winter at all, now. If I can swipe a little more lettuce and a few more carrots from that farm at the edge of the forest, we should be set!

(They "high five" each other.)

Mommy Mouse Mom Power!

Character Education Book of Plays
Elementary Level

THE BIG SWITCHEROO

Mama Rabbit Let's see if we have enough mom power to carry all of this into the pantry. Ready? Lift!

(MOMMY MOUSE, MOM SQUIRREL and MAMA RABBIT lift their bags again and slowly exit.)

Earl Squirrel Those bags look heavy!

Alvin Chipmunk The moms can hardly carry them.

Skippy That's great, though, isn't it, guys?

Jumpy What do you mean?

Skippy Well, if they're having a hard time carrying their bags and boxes, that means . . .

All Kids Lots of food for US!

(The KIDS "high five" each other and slap each other on the back.)

Double Click Mouse Oh well . . . back to the book.

Bouncy And back to Bunny.

Springy Here comes her boyfriend, Ben! Bunny and Ben, the perfect couple.

Jumpy I think they should go on a picnic!

(All KIDS resume their activities. SILVER FOX can't keep quiet on the sidelines.)

Silver Fox Can you believe they didn't help their mothers carry in that food for the winter?!

Respect Raccoon Just wait a minute, Silver, ol' pal, it's gonna get real interesting in a minute.

(Enter GRANDPA RABBIT, PAWPAW CHIPMUNK, DAD SQUIRREL and DADDY MOUSE.)

Pawpaw Chipmunk *(as though it is the end of a story)* And then I said to him, "Get outta the way, sonny, and let an expert do the job!" *(he laughs, and so do the other MEN.)* Yeah, that's what I said, all right. "Let an expert do the job!"

Dad Squirrel *(with affection)* Pawpaw Chipmunk, that is one of my favorite stories.

Grandpa Rabbit *(hard of hearing)* What?! Eh? Did somebody tell a good story?

THE BIG SWITCHEROO

Daddy Mouse	*(raising his voice a bit)* Pawpaw Chipmunk told his story about the goose, Grandpa Rabbit! I'm sorry you didn't hear it . . . but I bet he'll tell it again soon!
Dad Squirrel	Yep, I bet he will.
Daddy Mouse	I'll bet, I'll just bet.
Grandpa Rabbit	What? Who's all wet?
Dad Squirrel	Nobody's all wet, Grandpa Rabbit, but we're all going to be if we don't fix the holes in the tree!
Daddy Mouse	That's for sure. Those woodpeckers have done some damage this year! I'll bet they have pecked a hundred holes in our tree!
Dad Squirrel	You figure?
Daddy Mouse	I reckon.
Pawpaw Chipmunk	That reminds me of the time I was crouched beside a hollow log, and who should come along but an old porcupine!
Grandpa Rabbit	Old Frankenstein?! Did he say Frankenstein? Are you telling horror stories, Pawpaw Chipmunk?
Dad Squirrel	No, Grandpa, he said "porcupine." But before we let him tell that story, let's round up some kids.

(The KIDS have been intent on their games and book, but now look up with expressions of dread on their faces.)

Double Click Mouse	Did he just say "some kids"?
Earl Squirrel	I think so. Just keep reading, maybe they'll forget us.
Dad Squirrel	Sorry, Earl, it won't be that easy. Come on, you guys—we need some help. Woodpeckers have pecked lots of holes in the trunk of the tree. If we want to stay warm and dry all winter, we need to get out there and fill the holes with some pine sap and molasses.
Daddy Mouse	But Dad Squirrel and I can't do it alone, and some of us *(indicating GRANDPA RABBIT and PAWPAW CHIPMUNK)* are getting a little "on in years" to be climbing around too

Character Education Book of Plays
Elementary Level

Narrator: much. So come on—it'll be great. We'll work together—we'll share stories of the good old days . . .

Hoppy Save me! I'm having a heart attack!

Dad Squirrel We need your help, kids. Every last one of you. Now, we're going to go on out—you guys put away your dolls and book and join us outside. Come on, Grandpa Rabbit! Pawpaw Chipmunk!

Pawpaw Chipmunk Speaking of woodpeckers, you'll never believe this story. There was this woodpecker named Gladys . . .

Grandpa Rabbit Did you say horse radish? What about horse radish?

(GRANDPA RABBIT, PAWPAW CHIPMUNK, DAD SQUIRREL and DADDY MOUSE exit, but stay in sight of the audience as they pantomime gathering up tools, buckets, etc. The KIDS group together in the center of the stage.)

Earl Squirrel What are we gonna do?

Alvin Chipmunk We're doomed!

Double Click Mouse A day with the old guys is like . . . like . . .

Hoppy It's like a day with the old guys!

Springy They'll talk all day about old times . . .

Jumpy And Pawpaw Chipmunk will tell all those stories . . .

Bouncy And we'll get stuck repairing the tree instead of doing anything fun! And you know it will take all day!

All Kids *(facing the audience, hands outstretched as though wishing for an answer from the world)* Why us?!

Respect Raccoon *(rising from his chair, dusting popcorn off his pants, and crossing to center)* All right, that's enough! Freeze!

(They do.)

Oh well wait, I guess you can drop your hands. Oh, and get the rest of the folks back out.

(The KIDS drop their hands and all other cast members timidly walk on-stage, looking out at the audience.)

THE BIG SWITCHEROO

Now everybody freeze.

(They do.)

What is wrong with this picture? The kids answer their parents and grandparents with words like "huh" and "what;" they won't lend a hand to help their moms carry heavy parcels . . .

Silver Fox   Of food!

Respect Raccoon   Right . . .

Silver Fox   For them!

Respect Raccoon   And they have no spirit of pitching in to help their dads and grandpas repair the tree . . .

Silver Fox   Where they live!

Respect Raccoon   And in fact, they gripe and complain about having to listen to their grandfathers' old stories.

Silver Fox   Something is missing here, RR.

Respect Raccoon   I can name that thing in one word—RESPECT.

Silver Fox   Respect! That's it! *(A pause, then)* What a coincidence that you're Respect Raccoon!

Respect Raccoon   *(amused at his friend)* Yes, Silver, that is a big coincidence! But I'm going to teach them a little lesson, with a big switcheroo! Watch this!

(As he recites the following chant, he waves his arms over the heads of the cast, or produces a magic pine bough if you like and waves it like a wand. As he chants, SILVER FOX trades some costume pieces between old and young cast members. He takes glasses or an apron off an old person and puts that item on a young person; takes a baseball cap off of a young character and puts it on one of the older characters, etc.)

RESPECT IS MISSING, OF THAT WE ARE SURE
THAT IS THE ILLNESS, AND I HAVE THE CURE

IF A MOUNTAIN IS HIGH, YOU JUST HAVE TO HIKE IT
LET THEM CHANGE PLACES AND SEE HOW THEY LIKE IT!

Character Education Book of Plays
Elementary Level

(He claps his hands and returns to his chair stage right. The cast members look dazed. The old people seem to straighten up and look youthful, and The KIDS seen to be a little stooped. They blink and look at each other, then EARL SQUIRREL speaks.)

Earl Squirrel Uh . . . say . . . we need to get to that tree repair . . .

Grandpa Rabbit *(rudely)* Huh?

Double Click Mouse He said . . . we need to get out there and repair the trunk . . .

Granny Rabbit *(also somewhat rudely)* Well . . . whatever!

Hoppy We'd better get hopping, everybody—there are big holes in the trunk that could let in cold air this winter!

Meemaw Chipmunk Holes in the trunk could let in cold air? DUH!

(MEEMAW CHIPMUNK and GRANNY RABBIT "high five" each other)

Dad Squirrel Gosh, we'd really like to help you guys . . . but . . . we've been thinking about playing a game of acorn soccer. We really want to play!

Daddy Mouse Come on—you know we need our exercise! We're growing mice!

Jumpy It seems to me you'll get plenty of exercise repairing the tree!

Pawpaw Chipmunk Well that just shows what you know! Nothing!

Alvin Chipmunk I was wondering if someone would go gathering strawberries with me. I saw a patch by the old fence, and we could collect quite a few . . .

Springy I'll go, Alvin—but they might be heavy . . . Mama Rabbit? Would you help us carry strawberries if we get some?

Mama Rabbit So sorry—I NEVER lift heavy things. It's bad for my manicure! *(Wiggles her fingers, showing off her nails)*

Hoppy Manicure! That's funny. That reminds me of the time when I was about your age . . .

(All of the characters who used to be old start to ad-lib about how they'd love to stay and listen to the story, oops, gotta run, we'll be seeing ya, etc., looking at their watches)

Earl Squirrel Um . . . could I see you . . . uh . . . grown-ups . . . over here please?

THE BIG SWITCHEROO

(All the characters who used to be KIDS and are now GROWN-UPS gather with EARL stage left. The rest of the characters sit down, and pantomime reading, playing or talking among themselves.)

Earl Squirrel	Something very weird has happened, you guys! They've turned into us . . .
Skippy	And what's worse . . . we've turned into them!
Bouncy	This is horrible!
Double Click Mouse	Here's the worst thing, though—I can't believe how they're talking to us and how they're acting!
Hoppy	No kidding! Refusing to help us repair the tree . . .
Alvin Chipmunk	Not being willing to help us carry in heavy strawberries . . .
Springy	That THEY WILL want to eat later!
Jumpy	And the WAY they answer us! Words like "huh"!
Earl Squirrel	And "whatever"!
All Kids	And . . . "DUH"!
Double Click Mouse	They sound like . . . they sound like . . .
All Kids	They sound like us.
Hoppy	Gosh, I feel terrible.
Springy	Is that how we really sound? Is that how we've been talking to our sweet old Granny and Grandpa Rabbit?
Bouncy	It must be! It sure sounds familiar!
Skippy	We wouldn't help the moms with the stuff they gathered—we just kept right on playing Bunnies.
Alvin Chipmunk	And we couldn't put down our People-morphs long enough to say "please" or "thank you" for cookies that the grannies baked!
Earl Squirrel	I have to admit that I've always enjoyed the old guys' stories! Sometimes they're pretty funny—and they always teach me a little bit about what it was like when they were our age! I just pretended not to like them so I'd seem cool in front of you guys.

THE BIG SWITCHEROO

Double Click Mouse — I've been so mean—I never want to listen—and I sure didn't want to be stuck repairing the tree all day.

Alvin Chipmunk — We've been so crummy!

All The Rabbit "Children" — We deserve to be stew!

Earl Squirrel — No, nobody deserves to be stew, but maybe we deserve a second chance. Say—where's that Raccoon guy?

(SILVER FOX elbows RESPECT RACCOON in the side.)

Silver Fox — I think they mean you, RR!

Respect Raccoon — *(Crossing over to Earl and the others)* Yes, my elderly friends, what can I do for you?

Double Click Mouse — Sir, we realize how rotten we've been.

Hoppy — We really do love our parents and grandparents and we didn't mean to treat them so badly.

Jumpy — It was just like a bad habit that we picked up—and then didn't know how to put down!

Bouncy — But now we understand, and we're going to do better, we promise!

Earl Squirrel — Will you change us back? Please?

Respect Raccoon — I might be able to . . . if I think you realize what was missing in the way you treated your elders!

Springy — Well . . . niceness . . .

Skippy — Love wasn't missing, but it was hiding pretty well.

Respect Raccoon — One word will sum it up! What do you show when you speak nicely to your parents? What do you show when you listen politely to the stories your grandfather shares? What do you show when you help them with things they are not able to do so well anymore?

Silver Fox — *(Bursting out in song, as though not able to keep quiet another minute)* R - E - S - P - E - C - T! Find out what it means to me! *(He sings the first line of Aretha Franklin's famous song, Respect.)*

THE BIG SWITCHEROO

Respect Raccoon	Stop that, Silver! That's not a song in our play . . .
Silver Fox	Sorry, RR.
Respect Raccoon	He's right, though. It's called respect, and it's something your elders have earned by their love for you and the way they treat you kids, not just their age. Now come on.

(He leads the former KIDS to join the rest of the cast. As he chants, the young and old characters trade costume pieces back with affection, giving each other hugs as they do.)

> I THINK WE'VE ALL LEARNED A LESSON TODAY
> AS WE WATCHED, AND PERFORMED IN OUR LITTLE PLAY
>
> I'VE RESTORED PEACE TO THIS ANGRY MOB
> RESPECT RACCOON HAS DONE HIS JOB! BYE BYE!

(He salutes and exits. SILVER FOX lingers, waving at the audience and seeming reluctant to exit).

Granny Rabbit	Hooray! We're back to our old selves . . . and in my case, I do mean old!
Skippy	We're so sorry, Granny Rabbit! We'll never treat you with disrespect again!

(The four families divide into their groups and have family group hugs.)

Dad Squirrel	It looks like that guy taught us all a lesson.
Daddy Mouse	Say . . . who was that masked man? *(RESPECT RACCOON sticks his head back on-stage, and calls to SILVER FOX)*
Respect Raccoon	Hi ho—Silver! Away!

(The cast laughs and hugs as SILVER FOX exits with RESPECT RACCOON. Then, the two re-join the cast and all wave and call "Goodbye!" to the audience.)

Character Education Book of Plays
Elementary Level

Oh, No, You're Kidding!

A Mini-Play About
Respect

Character Education Book of Plays
Elementary Level

Oh, No, You're Kidding!

CAST

Jensen

K.L.

Jacky

Grandma

Mrs. Wright

Jessie's Mother

Mandy Sue's Mother

Mandy Sue

Oh, No, You're Kidding!

Notes to the Teacher/Director

The Big Switcheroo deals with the respect which young people should feel and demonstrate toward their elders; *Oh, No, You're Kidding!* deals with a different, but no less important, kind of respect. This play addresses gossiping.

Oh, No, You're Kidding! is a light-hearted, almost farcical short play in which one phone call leads to another, which leads to another, and so on. What starts out as a rumor about one character (Mandy Sue) failing to turn in a book report and making a zero becomes a wild tale about Mandy Sue and her friend Jessie running away with clowns to join the circus and ride on the backs of elephants. The message is clear—when we repeat information without knowledge of the truth, the facts can become distorted quickly.

Properties, Scenery, Costumes

This is a quick-and-easy play with no scenery and no special costumes, with the possible exception of some costuming of Grandma and the mothers. They can add baby powder to their temples, a pair of reading glasses, a shawl, and perhaps a skirt or house dress rather than school clothes. You need only two telephones (and some actors with a spirit of fun!). Keep the pace brisk and be creative with your telephone ring. The ring can be recorded or performed live by an actor.

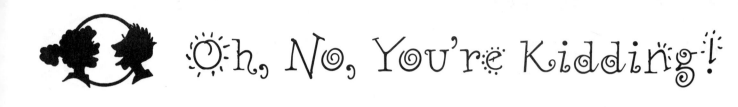

Teaching Materials to Accompany *Oh, No, You're Kidding!*

There is a time-honored game which your cast may enjoy playing before working on this play. Some people call it "Telephone," some call it "Telegraph," and some call it "Rumors."

Boys and girls sit in a circle, and the first person whispers a message to the person to his or her left. The message can be something simple such as "I like to braid my hair." Each person whispers it to his neighbor, in turn, and the final person in the circle speaks aloud the end result—usually something quite different than the original message! ("I rode a bike and ate a bear!")

Discuss with your cast that, although this is a harmless game, a cruel and/or untruthful message can be passed through a school, neighborhood, town, or even country in much the same way; the story changes and becomes more distorted as it is passed on. Urge students to refrain from passing on gossip, especially if it is juicy enough to make them say, "Oh, no, you're kidding!"

58

Oh, No, You're Kidding!

A Mini-Play About Respect

(When the play begins, there are two telephones on stage. They can be on desks, on TV trays, on two boxes, etc. One phone rings—by either a recorded sound effect, or perhaps an actor who sits on one side of the stage and says "RING!" loudly. When the first phone rings, JENSEN enters and answers.)

Jensen   Hello? Oh, hi, Sarah. What?! Oh, no, you're kidding! Mandy Sue forgot to hand in her book report? And she made a zero? That's terrible! And what? On no, you're kidding! And she's been too afraid to tell her mother, because she just knows she'll be grounded from the phone for the weekend? Well, I have to go call K.L. Bye!

(Phone rings. K.L. enters and answers.)

K. L.   Hello?

Jensen   K.L.?

K. L.   Speaking.

Jensen   Hi, it's Jensen.

K. L.   Hi, Jensen.

Jensen   You'll never guess what happened. Sarah called and told me that Mandy Sue forgot to hand in her book report and she made a zero! And she's grounded from the phone for the next six weeks!

K. L.   Oh, no, you're kidding! That's terrible!

Jensen   I know!

K. L.   Thanks for telling me. I'd better call Jacky. He'll want to hear this.

Jensen   OK. Bye.

(JENSEN and K.L. hang up. JENSEN exits. K.L. dials the phone. It rings. JACKY enters and answers.)

Oh, No, You're Kidding!

Jacky Hello?

K. L. Jacky?

Jacky Hey, K. L.

K. L. Hey. Listen, you'll never guess. Mandy Sue made a zero on a math paper and her parents have grounded her for the rest of the year! She can't talk on the phone or go anywhere!

Jacky Oh, no, you're kidding! She can't even go to the circus Saturday for Jessie's birthday?

K. L. No! Absolutely not! No circus for Mandy Sue!

Jacky Well, if Mandy Sue can't go to the circus, I don't know if I want to go. Maybe I'll go to my grandmother's house Saturday instead. She invited me. See you, K.L. I have to go call my grandmother.

K. L. OK, bye.

(JACKY and K.L. hang up. K.L. exits. JACKY dials the phone. It rings. GRANDMA enters and answers the phone.)

Grandma Hello? Who's there?

Jacky *(Speaking loudly because GRANDMA is hard of hearing)* HEY, GRANDMA! IT'S ME, JACKY!

Grandma Who?

Jacky JACKY, YOUR GRANDSON!

Grandma Hello, Jacky, my boy!

Jacky HI, GRANDMA. LISTEN—I WAS GOING TO THE CIRCUS WITH MY FRIEND JESSIE, BUT NOW I'M NOT BECAUSE MANDY SUE FORGOT HER BOOK REPORT, AND SHE GOT IN TROUBLE. SO, I CAN COME OVER SATURDAY IF YOU STILL WANT ME TO.

Grandma Oh, no, you're kidding! That's great news! Will you mow my yard for me?

Oh, No, You're Kidding!

Jacky	YES, GRANDMA, I'LL MOW YOUR YARD.
Grandma	Alright. See you then.
Jacky	BYE.
Grandma	Goodbye.

(They hang up. JACKY exits. GRANDMA dials the phone. It rings. MRS. WRIGHT enters and answers.)

Mrs. Wright	Hello?
Grandma	Hello? Mrs. Wright?
Mrs. Wright	IS THAT YOU, JACKY'S GRANDMA?
Grandma	*(aside, to audience)* Can't a woman have a name around here? *(back to the phone)* Yes, it's me. Listen, tell your son . . . what's his name? Oh yeah, Jared—tell Jared that he doesn't need to mow my yard after all on Saturday because my grandson, Jacky, is going to do it.
Mrs. Wright	JACKY? DOESN'T HE HAVE A BIRTHDAY PARTY TO GO TO FOR JESSIE?
Grandma	No, I think she got in trouble for not handing in some school-work and her mother has made her join the circus.
Mrs. Wright	JESSIE'S MOTHER MADE HER JOIN THE CIRCUS? OH, NO! YOU'RE KIDDING!
Grandma	Yes, that's right. Jessie and Mandy Sue both. Joining the circus, they are going to walk the tightrope and then hang from the flying trapeze!
Mrs. Wright	*(gasping)* WITH NO CIRCUS TRAINING.
Grandma	Well, I guess they will hand in their schoolwork on time from now on, won't they?
Mrs. Wright	I GUESS THEY WILL! WHAT A HARD LESSON TO LEARN. WELL, I'D BETTER GO AND CALL JESSIE'S MOTHER.
Grandma	All right. Bye.

Character Education Book of Plays
Elementary Level

Mrs. Wright   GOOD-BYE.

(GRANDMA and MRS. WRIGHT hang up. GRANDMA exits. MRS. WRIGHT dials the phone. It rings. JESSIE'S MOTHER enters and answers the phone.)

Jessie's mother   Hello?

Mrs. Wright   Hello? Is this Jessie's mother?

Jessie's mother   Yes. *(to audience)* Just once I wish someone would call me by my real name. *(back to phone)* Who's this?

Mrs. Wright   It's Mrs. Wright. I was just calling to say how awful I think it is that you're making Jessie join the circus.

Jessie's mother   What? What do you mean?

Mrs. Wright   I heard all about it. Just because of one school assignment . . . although, I must say that some of those little circus outfits are awfully cute! Some are pink and frilly and some are sparkly with sequins! Now that I think about it, Jessie and Mandy Sue ought to look really cute in those little costumes!

Jessie's mother   What on earth are you talking about? Never mind—I'd better call Mandy Sue's mother right away. Thank you for calling—good-bye.

Mrs. Wright   Goodbye.

(MRS. WRIGHT hangs up and exits. JESSIE'S MOTHER dials the phone. It rings. MANDY SUE'S MOTHER enters and answers the phone.)

Mandy Sue's mother   Hello?

Jessie's mother   Hello? Is this Mandy Sue's mother?

Mandy Sue's mother   *(Aside, to audience.)* I remember when I used to have a real name. *(back to the phone)* Yes, this is Mandy Sue's mother. Is this Jessie's mother?

Jessie's mother   Yes. I hear that our daughters are joining the circus!

Mandy Sue's mother   Oh, no, you're kidding!

Jessie's mother   That's what Mrs. Wright told me. She called me and said that

Oh, No, You're Kidding!

the girls are joining the circus and will be wearing glittery pink outfits and riding on the backs of elephants!

Mandy Sue's mother   No daughter of mine is riding on the back of an elephant without my permission! *(shouting to offstage area)* Mandy Sue! Mandy Sue, come in here please! *(back to the phone)* I'm going to go talk to my daughter. I'll call you back when I know something.

Jessie's mother   Alright. 'Bye.

(JESSIE'S MOTHER and MANDY SUE'S MOTHER hang up. JESSIE'S MOTHER exits. MANDY SUE enters.)

Mandy Sue   Yes, Mom? What's up?

Mandy Sue's mother   You, on the back of an elephant!

Mandy Sue   What?

Mandy Sue's mother   I understand that you and Jessie have met circus clowns and you have decided to run away with them and join the circus and ride on the backs of elephants who will be wearing glittery pink costumes!

Mandy Sue   Elephants in glittery pink costumes? Mom, are you all right?

Mandy Sue's mother   No! I'll never be all right again! My baby is joining the circus!

Mandy Sue   There, there, Mom, I'm not joining the circus. But I do have something to talk to you about . . . see, I had this book report due . . . and I forgot . . . and I made a zero!

Mandy Sue's mother   Oh, no, you're kidding. Well—can you hand it in tomorrow?

Mandy Sue   Yes. And I can do extra work to make up the grade.

Mandy Sue's mother   All right, Mandy Sue. Hand it in, do the extra work and everything will be all right. Now, about this circus . . .

Mandy Sue   *(exiting, excitedly.)* Can we talk about it later, Mom? I have to go call Sarah!

Character Education Book of Plays
Elementary Level

What A Tangled Web . . .
A Play About
Honesty

Character Education Book of Plays
Elementary Level

What A Tangled Web . . .

CAST

Ann Arachnid

Mark Barkley

Mary Grace Barkley

Sam Turner, *Mark's friend*

Mom

The Spider Chorus

What A Tangled Web . . .

Notes to the Teacher/Director

Mark never should have listened to his friend Sam! When Mark accidentally tosses his baseball into a box of his mother's ceramics, Sam talks him into blaming his little sister, Mary Grace. Mark follows Sam's advice. He tells a lie which results in another lie, and the cycle continues. The old saying, "What a tangled web we weave, when first we practice to deceive," is clearly demonstrated as Mark tries to avoid getting in trouble. Ann Arachnid, a spider, reveals to the audience that every time a boy or girl deceives someone, a spider gets tangled up in her web. She explains, "Kids don't have webs, so they can't get tangled up in them—it's up to us poor helpless spiders!"

As Ann gets increasingly more tangled on the sidelines, the lies continue until Mark realizes he has to confess to see if he can undo the damage he has done. When he confesses, Mark learns a lesson about honesty. He learns that it may just be the best policy!

This is a short, fun play with some wonderful acting opportunities in several of the roles. The Spider Chorus can be as large or small as you like, depending upon the number of children you need to include.

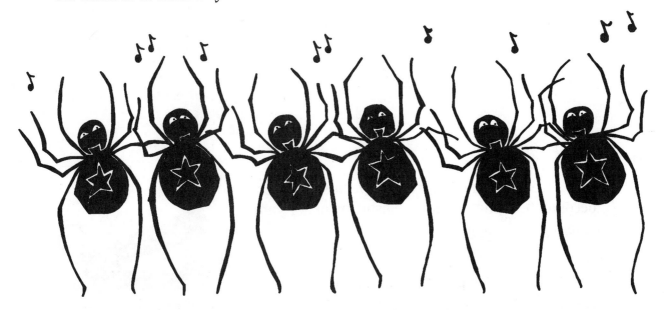

As in the play *The Big Switcheroo*, there are scenes in which a character (Ann) will remain on stage, but will not be the focus of the audience's attention. You may wish to make sure your actress understands the concept of "upstaging." Remind her

that she should react to the action on stage in small, silent ways. Ann should only speak out when she has scripted lines. (See *Notes to the Teacher/Director* for *The Big Switcheroo* for more discussion of this concept.)

The following words are used in the play. They may be new to your cast members. A vocabulary worksheet follows with some exercises which will help familiarize your students with these terms.

confusing

heed

ferocious

furious

arachnid

innocent

address (in this case, meaning "to speak to")

humorous

deceive

mature

disappointed

Properties

- Ann's web (which can be a Halloween spider web decoration, a length of rope, elastic, twine, or yarn)
- A baseball and glove
- A soccer ball
- A box with broken pieces of ceramics inside
- A purse and car keys for Mom, if you like

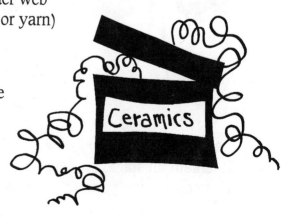

What A Tangled Web . . .

Scenery

What a Tangled Web . . . has minimal scenic requirements. You may choose to put a chair or stool to the side of the acting area so that Ann may have a seat when she is not the focus of the play. Most of the action takes place outside close to Mark's front porch. His stray pitch hits the box of ceramics on the porch. You will need to provide a place for this pitch to land that is not visible to the audience. Some scenic bushes could be constructed out of something sturdy, such as plywood, or something easy and available, such as posterboard or cardboard. Line up two or three bushes, and have a stagehand crouch behind them to catch Mark's pitch. (You could attach these shrubs to the front of teacher's desk and have your stagehand/catcher masked behind it.)

Sound Effects

Although not crucial by any means, it might be fun to include recorded sound effects and music at a few points in the play. First, Mark remarks to Mary Grace that he thinks he hears an ice cream truck. You may wish to record the music box melody of an ice cream truck, or seek out a pre-recorded sound effects record. Later, when the ball smashes Mom's box of ceramics, a pre-recorded crash (perhaps very exaggerated) would not only be humorous, but would also help advance the plot. Finally, when Ann and the Spider Chorus sing their song, Ann has the line "Hit it, boys!" It would be fun if some recorded accompaniment began to play at that point.

Technically, these sound effects could be accomplished in any of several ways. Ideally, your performance location is a lovely, well-equipped auditorium with a built-in, state-of-the-art sound system. If this is the case, simply find out whether a cassette tape or CD is preferred, and start recording. More likely, the site of your production will be your classroom or church activity room, in which case you can bring a portable CD player or tape recorder and have a class member punch the button. (It might be funny if he or she was in full view of the audience, especially when Ann says "Hit it, boys!")

The only necessary sound effect is the crashing of the ceramics. If sound effect recordings are unavailable, you could have a hidden cast member simply shake up a box of something that would sound like rattling broken pieces!

Character Education Book of Plays
Elementary Level

What A Tangled Web . . .

Costumes

The costume for Ann Arachnid will be fun and challenging. Dress her in a solid color, such as brown or black. (Since she refers to her mother, the black widow, you may wish to choose a black outfit and cut the identifying hourglass shape out of red and attach it to her torso.) Ann can wear sweats, leotards, matching pants and t-shirt, or dress; anything will be fun and fine.

In addition to places for your actress's two arms and two legs, the costume will need an additional four arms. This can be done by cutting sleeves out of old shirts from home, stuffing them with cotton or rags, then sewing them onto the costume. Ann may wish to wear dark gloves on her hands, and sew four more gloves onto the additional arms. (Since she will be belting out a jazzy number in the course of the play, she may prefer slinky black gloves from a costume store.) Since Ann has the line "Did I wear high heels and lose my balance?" you may also wish to provide her with an outrageous pair of red or black high heels, and change her line to "Did I lose my balance on my high heels?" The same sort of idea will work for the Spider Chorus, but Ann should have something to make her costume unique.

Mark and Sam should be wearing the casual clothes that boys wear when they are not in school. They might choose baseball jerseys of their favorite pro teams. (They are not on the way to their own game, so a uniform is not needed.) Toward the end of the play, when Mark comes in with his song lyric, "But tonight I'm playin' soccer for the Lady Bugs!," it would be fun to have him squeezed into a small red soccer jersey. (He has time to make a change while Ann and Sam have their scene.)

Mary Grace, of course, should wear a full soccer uniform in Lady Bug red.

Mom should be dressed casually; she did think she was on the way to the craft fair. She could wear a blue jean skirt, jeans or khakis, and a blouse or sweater. Of course, a pair of glasses or a little baby powder at the temples will age Mom a bit.

What A Tangled Web . . .

Teaching Materials to Accompany *What A Tangled Web . . .*

Class Discussion

1. Present the following questions for discussion:
   - When Sam advised Mark to blame the broken ceramics on Mary Grace, was he really being a good friend to Mark? If not, what advice would have been better?

   - Do you think Sam had bad feelings toward Mary Grace and wanted to make trouble for her, or was there some other reason he advised Mark to blame it on her?

2. See if your class/cast members can think of times when they were not quite truthful. Did the truth ever come out? If so, did things turn out worse than if they had been honest from the beginning? If the truth never came out, how did they feel?

"On Your Feet" Exercises

1. Sam and Mark are supposed to deliver several of their lines as a sports announcer would. How does a sports announcer speak? Have your class take turns reading aloud from a book or papers as if they were sports announcers. If an actor needs a little extra help for his or her voice, someone could tape a televised sporting event and bring it to school. (Exaggeration is encouraged!)

2. After making sure your class understands what it means to improvise a scene, try the following:
   a. Improvise the scene in which Mark tells Mom the truth. How would Mom react? Would she be angry, or would she also be happy that Mark is taking responsibility for his mistake?

   b. Create a scene in which Ann Arachnid tells someone (he or she need not be an actual character in the play) how she feels about people being dishonest.

   c. Improvise the scene in which Mark agrees to play soccer on Mary Grace's team, the Lady Bugs. Who probably came up with that idea—Mom or Mary Grace? How long do you think Mark resisted?

Vocabulary Worksheet

What A Tangled Web . . .

1. If someone gives **confusing** directions, are the directions easy or hard to understand?

   _____

2. Which of the following is a **ferocious** animal?

   _____ a. A turtle

   _____ b. A lion

   _____ c. A cow

3. Which of the following is *not* an **arachnid**?

   _____ a. A spider

   _____ b. A scorpion

   _____ c. A puppy

4. If an actor **addresses** the audience, what does he do to them?_____

5. If you attempt to **deceive** someone, are you being honest with that person? _____

Matching

Match the word with the definition which is most correct.

6. _____ disappointed   a. funny

7. _____ heed   b. not guilty

8. _____ furious   c. grown up

9. _____ innocent   d. very very angry

10. _____ humorous   e. pay attention to

11. _____ mature   f. sad because of how something turned out

What A Tangled Web . . .

A Play About Honesty

(ANN ARACHNID enters and faces the audience. She is a spider, and she is tangled up in a web.)

Ann　Hello, everybody, and how are you today? My name is Ann . . . Ann Arachnid. I'm a spider. And . . . maybe you can see . . . I am all tangled up in my web. How did this happen, you ask? Did I trip and fall in? Did I sleepwalk? Did I wear high heels and lose my balance? No, none of the above. See this guy here?

(Enter MARK, carrying a baseball glove and tossing a ball. He does not see the audience or ANN—he's in his own little baseball world.)

This is Mark. Mark is a good kid, really. He loves his mother and his father, remembers to feed his dog, and does his homework without being reminded too many times. Oh, and he has a little sister named Mary Grace.

(MARY GRACE enters, kicking a soccer ball.)

Mark　*(noticing his sister)* What do you want?

Mary Grace　I want to be an only child.

Mark　Same here!

Mary Grace　Too bad, too late, I'm here to stay.

Mark　Tough luck.

Mary Grace　Do you have a game tonight?

Mark　No. Do you big scary Lady Bugs have a soccer game?

Mary Grace　Yeah. We're playing the Pink Panthers.

Mark　They're gonna kill you! They do every time!

Mary Grace　No, they're not. Coach Rick says we can pound 'em into the ground!

Character Education Book of Plays
Elementary Level

What A Tangled Web . . .

Mark   You must have some new players.

Mary Grace   Are you kidding? I'm great, and my best friend Jenny is great. We don't need any new players—we have been practicing. *(makes a ferocious fist)* The Pink Panthers don't have a chance!

Mark   Dream on. *(listens to something)* Hey, I think I hear the ice cream truck! Want to go get an ice cream?

Mary Grace   Sure.

(They exit.)

Ann   See? Normal brother and sister. Anyway . . . the problem with my web . . . let's start at the beginning.
(She addresses a member of the audience)
Sir? Would you hold this, please?
(ANN gives the audience member the end of her web.)
Now hold on tight.
(She spins slowly, unwinding the web from around her, then she takes it from the audience member.)
Thank you very much.
(Stretching her various limbs)
That feels much better.

The problem with my web began with Mark. And a lie that he told. Is this confusing? Let me explain.
Have you ever heard the old saying "What a tangled web we weave when first we practice to deceive"? Well, here's how it works. When a kid deceives, or lies to someone, a spider somewhere gets tangled up in her web. I mean, kids don't have webs, so they can't get tangled up in them—it's up to us poor helpless spiders! It's a little like that angel getting his wings in that Christmas movie—every time a bell rings, an angel gets his wings—you know? Well, every time a kid deceives, a spider . . . you get the picture.

Anyway, one day Mark was tossing his baseball around with his friend Sam.

What A Tangled Web . . .

(ANN stands or sits at the side of the stage. Enter SAM and MARK, tossing the ball back and forth. The boys say the following lines as though they are sports commentators.)

Mark And he steps up to the mound—he has the look of a wild jungle beast in his eye . . .

Sam Sam Turner, his friend from fifth grade, is in the catcher's box. He gives Mark the sign . . . Mark throws . . . *(MARK throws the ball to SAM, who catches it.)* Stee-rike! The worthless batter is O-U-T outta here!

Mark The crowd goes wild! No one can believe it! He's struck out every single batter from the opposing team . . . which is named . . . uh . . .

Sam The Sniveling Mama's Babies!

Mark Yeah! The Sniveling Mama's Babies don't have a chance against the awesome power of Mark's amazing pitching!

(MARK pitches the ball again, this time out of the audience's sight, either offstage, behind the teacher's desk or behind some scenery. A loud crash is heard. SAM and MARK freeze.)

Sam *(running to the spot of the "crash.")* Oh Mark, what have you done now, you animal? He's tough . . . he's cool . . . he's . . . dead! His mother's going to kill him! *(SAM has picked up a box, filled with ceramic pieces. He re-enters, carrying it and shaking it slightly, perhaps picking one broken piece out of the box and showing it to MARK.)* It looks like his speed ball has done a number on . . .

Mark My mom's ceramics!

Sam His mom's ceramics.

Mark Oh, no! I AM dead!

Sam No one doubts the fury of Mark's mother when she finds the pieces of her ceramics, smashed like so many pieces of dreams . . .

Character Education Book of Plays
Elementary Level

What A Tangled Web . . .

Mark OK, Sam, that's good.

Sam Is his career in the major leagues finished? Or will this powerful pitcher be grounded for the rest of his life?!

Mark Sam, cut it out! I'm doomed! My mother made all these ceramics to sell at some craft fair this weekend—and she put them on the porch in this box and now . . .

(SAM, looking sad, shakes the box and rattles the pieces.)

Sam *(Continuing as sports commentator)* Would he have been a Hall-of-Famer? Would he have pitched in the World Series? We'll never know. His too-short career was ended by his mother when he smashed her ceramics— and she smashed him.

Mark OK, Sam, stop it! I'm in trouble here! *(He takes the box of ceramics.)* Maybe they're not too badly crunched . . . maybe I can glue them back together . . .

(Both boys look in at the pieces, look back at each other, and shake their heads sadly.)

Sam There's only one answer.

Mark What? I can't wait to hear this.

Sam Tell her your sister did it.

Mark I can't try to pin it on Mary Grace! What kind of a crummy brother do you think I am?

Sam The kind of crummy brother who's about to get grounded for at least this weekend, and probably all the way through next weekend when we badly need him to pitch for our team!

Mark But Mary Grace didn't do anything . . .

Sam And your mother won't be as hard on her! You know how it is with moms and sisters—sisters always get off easier!

What A Tangled Web . . .

Mom *(from offstage)* Mark? Mary Grace? Where is everyone? I need some help finding something.

(SAM and MARK scramble to hide the box of broken ceramics behind them as MOM enters.)

There you are. Oh, hi, Sam. Say, boys, I've lost something. I put a box of ceramics on the porch to dry because they were just a little bit wet—anyway, I can't seem to see them now and . . . wait . . . *(spying the box behind the boys)* that looks like the box behind you!

Sam Something terrible happened, Mrs. Barkley. I'm afraid there was an accident . . .

Mom What? Give me those . . . *(MOM snatches the box of ceramics and gasps.)* Oh, no! Look at this! They're all ruined!

Mark Mom, I can explain . . .

Mom I sure hope so, young man, because I was on my way to the craft fair with these!

Mark Well, Sam and I were throwing the ball back and forth . . .

Sam When Mary Grace came by . . .

(ANN begins to wrap the web around one of her legs.)

Ann It starts!

Mark Well, no, I mean . . .

Mom Mary Grace? Did Mary Grace do this?

Sam You know how she's always kicking that soccer ball around . . .

Mom Is that what happened? She kicked her soccer ball into the box?

What A Tangled Web . . .

Mark   Well . . .

Sam   *(Aside, to MARK)* Go ahead! She'll get off easy—you would be pounded!

Mark   Yes, Mom. Mary Grace . . . kicked her soccer ball into that box of ceramics.

Ann   *(tangling up in her web even more)* More fibs—more tangles!

Sam   Mrs. Barkley, I'm so sorry. Your poor ceramics! You must have worked so hard . . .

Mark   Sam, put a lid on it.

Mom   Well, I am certainly disappointed in Mary Grace. Not just because she ruined all my hard work, but she didn't even come and tell me. I'd better go find her. If you boys see her, tell her I'm looking for her.

Sam & Mark   OK!

(MOM exits, carrying the box of broken ceramics.)

Mark   That felt so creepy! I hated lying to Mom! And poor Mary Grace—what if she gets grounded from playing soccer tonight?

Sam   Relax! She won't get grounded from soccer. She'll just get scolded and told to be more careful. She's a girl! Girls have it easy!

Ann   *(Tangling up more)* Oh—that's a good one!

Mark   I guess . . .

Sam   Well, I gotta go home. See you later . . . *(speaking in sports commentator style again)* Mark Barkley . . . the wild beast with the wild ceramic-smashing pitching arm . . . what will he smash next? He's outta control . . .

(SAM exits. MARK remains on stage, sadly tossing his ball into his glove.)

What A Tangled Web . . .

Ann (*Limping to center stage, though it's getting harder to walk*) Here's the sad part. If he would stop lying right now, and go back to his mother and tell the truth, then I wouldn't be tangled up at all. Sure, his mother would be really mad at him for breaking the ceramics and blaming it on Mary Grace, but it's only going to get worse.

(ANN limps back to her side of the stage. MARK looks up as MARY GRACE enters, obviously upset.)

Mark Hey, MG—what's the matter?

Mary Grace The most awful thing! Somebody smashed Mom's ceramics—not me, I promise! But somebody told her it was me! Somebody told a huge lie! Who would do such a thing?

Mark (*hesitantly*) Well . . . I can't say for sure . . . but I think I saw Jenny talking to Mom.

Mary Grace Jenny? My best friend?

Ann (*becoming more and more tangled*) Oh, now here's some good tangling going on! Much more of this and I won't be able to scratch my nose!

Mark I don't know what they were talking about, but Mom pointed to the ceramics and Jenny . . . Jenny nodded her head and I think I heard her say "Mary Grace."

Mary Grace (*really upset now*) That is the worst thing I ever heard! Jenny is supposed to be my friend! Why would she tell such a lie? Well, I'll fix her! I'll go tell her mother . . . I'll tell her . . . something rotten! (*She storms off, furious.*)

Mark Oh, this lie just gets bigger and bigger, like Pinnochio's nose.

(MARK exits, sadly)

Character Education Book of Plays
Elementary Level

What A Tangled Web . . .

Ann   *(hopping and limping to center)* Well, as my mother, the black widow, used to say—when in doubt—sing! Hit it, boys!

(Musical accompaniment in, SPIDER CHORUS enters, as ANN sings)

Ann   TELL A LIE, TELL ANOTHER
HURT YOUR FRIEND, HURT YOUR MOTHER
ANOTHER FIB IS UP YOUR SLEEVE
WHAT A TANGLED WEB YOU WEAVE

Spider Chorus   BROTHER MARK, YOU MUST BE TRUE
COME, DO WHAT YOU GOTTA DO
DON'T LET MARY TAKE THE RAP
YOUR BUDDY SAM IS SUCH A SAP!

Ann   A SPIDER WEB IS TOUGH AND STRONG
BUT TELLING LIES IS OH SO WRONG
I KNOW THAT YOU'RE COVERIN' UP —
BUT LOOK A'HERE—I'M TANGLED UP!

Spider Chorus   LISTEN NOW AND HEED HER WORDS
THE BEST ADVICE YOU'VE EVER HEARD
DON'T YOU BLAME YOUR SIS NO MO'
HONESTY'S THE WAY TO GO!

All Spiders   TELL THE TRUTH—YEAH!

(THE SPIDER CHORUS bows and exits. ANN remains center stage.)

Ann   I'm going to be so disappointed in Mark if he doesn't do the right thing. *(sees MARK entering.)* Shhh—here he comes. *(ANN hobbles over to the side of the stage.)*

(MARK and SAM enter.)

Mark   I thought I would feel guilty—but I really don't! Sure, I broke that stuff—but Mary Grace has done plenty that she didn't get in trouble for!

Sam   You know that's right!

Mark   I'm the good brother . . .

What A Tangled Web . . .

Ann   I feel a tangle coming on!

Mark   . . . and I'm always getting busted for this and that. I think . . .

Sam   *(as sports announcer)* Mark, trying to feel a little guilty, but fighting it off! It's this kind of fearless courage that has put him at the top of his game . . .

(Enter MARY GRACE, sniffling.)

Mary Grace   Well, I did it!

Mark   What did you do?

Mary Grace   I went right over to Jenny's house and told her mother that Jenny broke Mom's ceramics!

Ann   *(tangling up further)* Round and round this lie goes— where it stops, nobody knows!

Mary Grace   Jenny's mother was furious! She made Jenny come out and apologize . . . and . . . Jenny looked really innocent, but I'm sure that was just an act . . . anyway, her mom said she couldn't play soccer with the Lady Bugs for two weeks!

Mark   Really?

Mary Grace   Yeah. So . . . Jenny gets what she deserves!

Mark   *(looking miserable)* Um . . . MG . . . you know, maybe she didn't really . . .

Sam   *(As announcer, a little more softly, so that MARY GRACE won't hear)* Oh, no! He's weakening! Will Mark the Man turn into Mark the Wimp and confess?

Mark   I'd hate it if you got Jenny in trouble by mistake . . .

Mary Grace   What do you mean "by mistake"? Did you hear her blame me or not?

Sam   He's on the hot seat now for sure, ladies and gentlemen! His career as a brother could be over right now!

What A Tangled Web . . .

Mark   Oh, Mary, I can't keep this up. I broke the ceramics with my baseball. I told Mom you did it —

Mary Grace   You creep!

Sam   Indeed, sports fans, Mark Barkley has just been named Creep of the Year in the brother competition . . .

Mark   I'm so sorry. I was wrong, wrong, wrong. And I don't have any good excuse, except I listened to bad advice from a friend. *(Looks at SAM.)*

Sam   *(looking right and left, innocently)* Who me? I was just . . . just . . .

Mark   *(as an announcer)* For once, sports fans, Sam has nothing to say! *(Turning back to MARY GRACE.)* Come on. Let's go talk to Jenny and her mother first, then Mom. We're going to get this all straightened out. I guess I'm going to be spending the rest of my weekend making ceramics! And heaven knows what else she'll do to me!

(MARK and MARY GRACE exit. SAM crosses to ANN)

Sam   Well, Ms. Arachnid—looks like you're about to be untangled.

(SAM takes one end of the "web" and untangles ANN.)

Ann   Thanks, Sam. Now, do me a favor and don't talk Mark into telling any more fibs.

Sam   Me? I never would. I'm an honest boy. I'm loyal. I'm humorous, yet not a pest. I'm . . .

(As he talks, ANN begins to wind herself back up in her web.)

Ann   Oh, what a tangled web I'm in—when I talk to Mark's best friend!

(SAM looks at the audience with a VERY innocent face. Musical accompaniment begins. THE SPIDER CHORUS, MARY GRACE and MOM enter.)

What A Tangled Web . . .

Ann   *(Tossing off her web once and for all)*
NO MORE LIES, DON'T TELL ANOTHER
MARK CAME CLEAN, HE TOLD HIS MOTHER
NO MORE FIBS ARE UP HIS SLEEVE
NO MORE TANGLED WEBS TO WEAVE

(Spider Chorus echoes)   *(you weave)*

Ann
(Spider Chorus echoes)   BROTHER MARK HAS NOW BEEN TRUE
HE DID WHAT HE HAD TO DO
FOUND HIMSELF IN QUITE A JAM
NEVER SHOULDA' LISTENED TO HIS FRIEND SAM

Mom   I'M PROUD HE FINALLY TOLD THE TRUTH
HE WAS MATURE, DESPITE HIS YOUTH
HE OWES HIS SISTER LOTS OF HUGS —

Mark   *(entering in Lady Bug soccer uniform)*
BUT TONIGHT I'M PLAYIN' SOCCER FOR THE LADY
BUGS!

Cast   LISTEN NOW AND HEED OUR WORDS
THE BEST ADVICE YOU'VE EVER HEARD
DON'T BE TELLIN' LIES NO MO'
HONESTY'S THE WAY TO GO!
TELL THE TRUTH—YEAH!

Character Education Book of Plays
Elementary Level

What A Tangled Web . . .

"Tell The Truth"

Lyrics by Judy Truesdell Mecca

Music by Jenifer Truesdell Christman

Character Education Book of Plays
Elementary Level

85

Talk About Responsibility!

A Play About Responsibility

Character Education Book of Plays
Elementary Level

Talk About Responsibility!

CAST

Audience Members

Stage Manager

Kay Nine, *host of the show*

Mama Cat Elliott, *a cat*

Hannah, *Mama Cat's girl*

Glubby the Goldfish

Gregory, *Glubby's boy*

Gregory's Mom

Newspaper

Homework

Herman the Hermit Crab

Pandra, *Herman's girl*

Talk About Responsibility!

Notes to the Teacher/Director

It's the Kay Nine Show, and pets are being given the opportunity to speak out! It seems that kids far and wide are accepting the responsibility of having a pet, but they are dropping the ball when it comes to the details like feeding and cleaning.

The play is structured as though it is a taping of this talk show. There is even a "word from the sponsor," regarding the responsibility for homework and other commitments. In the end, the message is clear—kids must stand up and start taking responsibility!

This is a short, fun, easily-produced play in which many children can be in the spotlight, with no one cast member having a huge quantity of lines to memorize. Some characters are people, some are animals—and there is a lot of room for creativity in costuming, as well as in characterization.

There can be as many Audience Members as you like, though only one actually has scripted lines, all can ad-lib and react to the action on stage.

The following words are included in the script and may be new to your students:

enthusiastically

demonstrating

hysterically

timidly

hesitantly

imaginary

brochure

accusingly

A worksheet is included to help familiarize your cast members with these words.

Talk About Responsibility!

Properties

None needed this time!

Scenery

The play takes place on the set of a daytime television talk show. You will need a prominently featured chair or desk for host Kay Nine, and then arrange classroom or folding chairs to represent the typical talk show sofa. Your challenge in staging this show will be in arranging the Audience Members who are part of the cast so that their facial expressions are visible to the real audience members. You might consider dividing the Audience Members into two sections, stage left and right of the action. Then, the real audience becomes the other third of the studio audience, but the cast members are still visible.

Costumes

Several of the characters in this play are obviously animals, but don't panic! There are many ways to represent the animals being portrayed without renting expensive costumes or causing parents who sew to run for cover.

Your Audience Members can be animals or people. It might be fun to have an all-animal audience, with Audience Members wearing solid color sweats, then suggesting dog ears (made of dark colored socks) and drawing on a dog nose with theatrical make-up or eyeliner, or making cat ears out of construction paper and affixing them with bobby pins. Cat whiskers can also be drawn on with eye pencils. Let students come up with creative costumes—for example, a brightly-colored parrot, who might wear a tropical shirt while sporting a construction-paper beak held in place by a slender piece of elastic (stapled snugly on both sides). How about a hamster, with small brown

Talk About Responsibility!

construction paper ears and whiskers? Maybe an all-white sweats outfit suggests a cockatiel with a giant plume of craft store feathers attached to the front of your actor's head with bobby pins or a head band. Or—of course—they can all be normal people and wear regular street clothes . . .

Stage Manager should probably be a dog. (See above for dog costume suggestions.) Be sure to give him a pair of important-looking headphones to wear.

Kay Nine must, of course, be a dog. Dress her in solid brown sweats, or white sweats with brown marker spots or construction paper blotches. Fashion some ears for Kay Nine out of some of dad's brown socks, and attach them to a headband. Give your actor a few whiskers and maybe a belt or piece of fake fur attached to the seat of her pants as a tail.

Mama Cat Elliott should be the grandest cat on television! Choose your own color scheme (but make sure it's elegant!) such as solid white with pink trim or perhaps even something silver or something that sparkles. She should probably wear something more feminine than sweats—maybe a leotard and tights outfit or some other dance attire. Or—maybe a lovely formal gown from mom's dress-up collection or a local thrift shop! Give her some triangular kitty ears (made of construction paper or fake fur scraps) and attach them to her head with bobby pins. Eye pencil whiskers are a must, and you might also wish to find some old gloves (or invest in some long gold lamé or white) and attach fake fingernails for claws, painted gold or bright pink—something fashionably fabulous. Mama Cat may wish to have a tail made out of some coordinating fake fur, or a gold or pink patent leather belt from the thrift store or mom's wild belt collection.

Hannah, Gregory, and Pandra should all wear normal clothes. Gregory's Mom should also wear normal mom clothing. You may wish to add glasses or some baby powder gray hair.

Character Education Book of Plays
Elementary Level

Talk About Responsibility!

Glubby the Goldfish should, of course, wear gold. This can be sweats, or something shiny gold, like a dance costume. (Maybe your actor's mom sews and could make a shiny gold jacket or shirt—it could be worn with white or black pants or jeans.) If his costume is thrift store fare, or about to be outgrown, maybe scales could be drawn on with a laundry marker.

Newspaper and Homework in the commercial will be fun to costume. For Newspaper, start with a vest (either an old one, a thrift store discard, or even one cut from sturdy brown paper). Then glue on articles cut from real newspapers. It might be fun to give him a hat with a sign saying PRESS sticking out of the brim, as in old movies. His pants should be white or black jeans.

Homework can also start with a disposable vest. What could be attached to represent homework? Small notebooks, pencils, maybe a school book cover or two. Perhaps Homework is very colorful, in contrast to Newspaper being basically black and white. Homework could also wear jeans or other dark colored pants.

Herman The Hermit Crab should wear a solid, neutral color sweats outfit—gray, brown, black or white. Attach a too-small shell to his or her back, either with hot melt glue or yarn. Represent his pinchers by giving him one normal glove or mitten, and one big oven mitt!

Talk About Responsibility!

Teaching Materials to Accompany *Talk About Responsibility!*

Class Discussion

As a class, discuss any responsibilities involving pet care that students or cast members have, or have had in the past. How are they doing? Do their parents have to remind them constantly to take care of their animals, or are they remembering on their own? Discuss the fact that the pets are dependent upon them in much the same way they are dependent upon their parents. What if Mom or Dad forgot to go to the grocery store? Most elementary school students are not able to get in the car and go buy dinner, in the same way that pets cannot take care of themselves. Compare students' needs for parent care with pets' needs for their young owners' care.

On a lighter note, have your class brainstorm to come up with additional 1-800 numbers for Newspaper and Homework to say to each other as they exit.

This play takes place on the set of a TV talk show. Have any of your class or cast members ever attended the taping of a television show? See if he or she would describe the experience to the class.

Writing Exercises

Have your class write one of the following:

1. A story about a boy (or girl) who has no responsibility at all! Mom does his homework for him, packs his backpack for him in the morning, and never asks for any help around the house. Now show him as an adult! What is he like?

2. A horror story in which, somehow, pets and kids are switched! Our heroine wakes up in her dog's house . . . or her cat's bed . . . what happens?

3. A letter from a pet to his master, letting the master know how he could do a better job.

Art Project

Have a pet accessory art day! Have boys and girls create animal ears, noses, tails, feathers, etc. Be sure to have lots of construction paper, pipe cleaners, fake fur, markers, feathers, scraps of material, glue, staples, and elastic on hand.

Talk About Responsibility!

1. If someone says "yes!" **enthusiastically**, this means that they:
   a. _____ seem to be very excited
   b. _____ do not want to speak up
   c. _____ are confused

2. Which of these is the best definition of the word **demonstrating**?
   a. _____ complaining
   b. _____ showing how to do something
   c. _____ behaving like a monster

3. Describe how someone would look who was laughing **hysterically**.

   _____

   _____

4. Which of these words has almost the same meaning as the word **timidly**?
   a. _____ loudly
   b. _____ angrily
   c. _____ shyly

5. If a person speaks **hesitantly**, is he very excited
   to talk, using a loud, almost shouting voice?   _____

6. **Imaginary** most nearly means:
   a. _____ colorful
   b. _____ not really there
   c. _____ dreamy

7. A **brochure** is:
   a. _____ a small printed booklet
   b. _____ a piece of jewelry
   c. _____ a television commercial

8. If someone speaks to you **accusingly**, what do they probably think?
   a. _____ that you are nice
   b. _____ that you have done something wrong
   c. _____ that you are in a disguise

Talk About Responsibility!

A Play About Responsibility

(The play begins as AUDIENCE MEMBERS enter and take their seats, talking among themselves about the live television show they are about to see taped. When they have all taken their seats, STAGE MANAGER enters and speaks to them.)

Stage Manager   Hello everyone, welcome to the show. I hope you didn't have to wait outside too long in the rain, but since you're not made of sugar, you didn't melt.

(AUDIENCE MEMBERS look at each other, rolling eyes, not appreciating STAGE MANAGER'S humor.)

Moving right along . . . when our host comes out, I want you all to cheer and clap and keep the energy level up, OK? Just remember . . . your tickets were free. Anyway, here she is, the star of our show, Kay Nine!

(AUDIENCE claps enthusiastically as KAY NINE, the show's host, enters. STAGE MANAGER runs back and forth in front of the audience, demonstrating silently how to clap and cheer. KAY takes center stage, waving to the audience. STAGE MANAGER moves off to one side.)

Kay   Hello, everyone, and welcome to the Kay Nine Show! I would like to say hello to those of you watching at home, and welcome to our studio audience. I hope you didn't have to wait outside too long in the rain— but since you're not made of sugar, hopefully you didn't melt!

(AUDIENCE MEMBERS laugh hysterically at the same joke, this time coming from KAY. STAGE MANAGER sticks his head back in briefly.)

Stage Manager   Hey! I said the same . . .

(He makes a gesture as if to say "Aw forget it," and returns to his offstage location.)

Talk About Responsibility!

Kay   Today's show deals with a serious problem among some of today's young people. That problem is . . . responsibility. What is it? Why is it important? Who has it and who doesn't? How do you spell it? We'll be answering these questions today, so let's get started. Our first guest is no stranger to mice, and certainly knows her way around a scratching post. Please help me welcome . . . Mama Cat Elliott!

(MAMA CAT ELLIOTT enters, twirling her tail and waving to the audience grandly. She takes her seat.)

Kay   Welcome, Miss Elliott—or may I call you Mama Cat?

Mama Cat Elliott   You may call me Miss Elliott—is that purr . . . fectly clear?

Kay   Er . . . yes . . . purr . . . fectly. Now, I understand that you're having trouble with your girl, is that right?

Mama Cat Elliott   Yes, that's right. It's my girl, Hannah—the one I let live with me? It's her job to feed me, to make sure I have water, and—this is embarrassing—to make sure my "special box" is clean, if you know what I mean.

Kay   We all have a "special box," Miss Elliott. Don't be embarrassed.

Mama Cat Elliott   Well, for some of y'all, that "special box" is the whole back yard, but don't get me started! Anyway, when I agreed to let Hannah take me home and be my girl, her mother said she had to take care of those jobs! And guess what—she forgets half the time!

Kay   You're kidding!

Talk About Responsibility!

Mama Cat Elliott	Honey, I wish! Her mother feeds me and gets me water most of the time—but that other thing—it's just too painful to talk about.
Kay	You're in for a surprise, Mama Cat Elliott, because we've brought your girl Hannah all the way from Asheville, North Carolina *(or insert local town here)* to work out your problems on today's show! Hannah, come on in!

(MAMA CAT ELLIOTT looks shocked. HANNAH enters timidly and takes her seat.)

Hannah	Hello, Ms. Nine. Hello, Mama Cat Elliott.
Mama Cat Elliott	*(Turning her back)* Humph!
Kay	Hello Hannah, and welcome to the show. Now, we understand that there is some problem about the things you're supposed to do for Mama Cat Elliott!
Hannah	Well . . . I guess so. And I mean to, I really do, but I just forget sometimes!
Mama Cat Elliott	More like EVERY time.
Hannah	But I'm so busy, Kay . . . and Mama Cat! I'm in Girl Scouts, I take tumbling . . . I have an Internet pen pal . . .
Mama Cat	Well, I have things to do, too! Naps to take, birds to chase, little catnip toys to bat around—but does that mean I forget to curl up on your lap and purr and rub up against your ankle? No! I always hold up my end of the deal.
Hannah	Aw, Mama Cat—I have homework all the time . . .
Mama Cat Elliott	*(Holding up a paw)* Girl, I want you to talk to the paw, 'cause the whiskers ain't twitchin'!

Character Education Book of Plays
Elementary Level

Talk About Responsibility!

Kay   Ladies and gentlemen of the audience, what do you think? If Hannah agreed to do certain things if she could have a cat . . . or rather, a cat could have her . . . she should do them, shouldn't she? Because they're her . . .

Audience   . . . RESPONSIBILITY!

Mama Cat Elliott   That's what I'm saying!

Hannah   You are all right, of course. This was the deal—and I haven't done my part. I'll do a better job from now on, Mama Cat! No more empty cat dishes or stinky . . .

Mama Cat Elliott   Oh, girl, don't even go there!

Hannah   I'll live up to my responsibility. You'll see.

(HANNAH and MAMA CAT ELLIOTT hug and move down to the end of the chairs.)

Kay   All right, a happy ending. Let's bring out our next guest . . . he's a terrific swimmer, and worth his weight in gold—help me welcome Glubby the Goldfish!

(Enter GLUBBY, nervously biting on his "nails" and waving hesitantly to the audience. He takes his seat.)

Kay   Glubby, welcome to the show.

Glubby   Thanks, Kay, I'm really pleased to have this chance to speak out.

Kay   And just what is your problem, Glubby? Tell us all about it.

Glubby   It's my boy—Gregory. His grandmother gave him some money . . . and he was allowed to buy anything he wanted from the dime store . . . and . . . he bought me . . .

Talk About Responsibility!

Kay But that's a good thing, isn't it? Surely it was crowded in that dime store fish tank!

Glubby Oh, don't get me wrong! It was great to have my own room! But once he got me home and dumped me out of the plastic bag into the bowl—he just forgot about me! He throws in a handful of food once in a while—and I have to remember not to eat it all at once—and the bowl is dirty—and there aren't any little castles to swim around in . . .
(bursts into tears)

Kay There, there, Glubby, I think we can help. Gregory—come on out!

(GREGORY enters, trying to look cool and unconcerned. He takes his seat.)

Hello, Gregory, and welcome to the show.

Gregory Hey, Kay, what's up? What's Glubby doin' here?

Glubby Trying to get some fair treatment, that's all!

Kay Glubby here feels that you forgot about him the minute you brought him home from the dime store. You should feed him a little every day, not a big glob when you think about it.

Gregory Hey, at least I feed him!

Glubby And you never wash my bowl—and there aren't any little pieces of coral or any plastic mermaids!

Gregory Do I look like a rich kid with a big allowance?

Glubby It's no use—he'll never change!

(GLUBBY falls over on the sofa and cries.)

(GREGORY'S MOM stands up and speaks out.)

*Character Education Book of Plays
Elementary Level*

Talk About Responsibility!

Gregory's Mom	Now you listen to me, Gregory!
Gregory	Mom, what are you doing here?
Gregory's Mom	Well. you won't listen to me at home—maybe you will listen to me on national television. You need to take better care of your pet! You brought him into this world—he didn't ask to leave that store!
Gregory	But Mom, I gave him a home . . .
Gregory's Mom	And it's filthy! What if I let our house get all slimy and stinky?! How would you like that?

(GLUBBY looks up, horrified at this idea.)

Gregory	I guess I wouldn't. I will take better care of Glubby.
Gregory's Mom	See that you do . . . because that little fish is your . . . *(turns to the audience and holds out her hands, inviting them to join her)*
Audience	. . . RESPONSIBILITY!
Gregory's Mom	Amen and hallelujah!

(She sits down.)

Kay	There you have it, Gregory! Do you think you can take better care of Glubby?
Gregory	Sure. Yeah, I guess so.
Glubby	Thank you, Gregory, that would really be great. Oh, and one more thing . . .
Gregory	What now? Do you want to watch the all-fish channel on cable every night?
Gregory's Mom	Watch it there, Mr. Smarty!
Gregory	Sorry . . .

Talk About Responsibility!

Glubby   It's my name . . . "Glubby." I mean, did you just try to come up with the dumbest sounding name in the world? Couldn't you call me . . . King Midas the Goldfish . . . or Goldfish Hawn . . .

Gregory   I give up . . .

Kay   Thank you, Glubby and Gregory! You look like you're on the right track. We'll be right back for our final guest after this word from our sponsor.

(AUDIENCE applauds. GREGORY and GLUBBY move down, and then everyone on stage freezes. Enter NEWSPAPER and HOMEWORK stage left.)

Newspaper   Hello, I'm your local newspaper.

Homework   And my name is Homework.

Newspaper   We're here to talk about . . . well . . . responsibility.

Homework   *(to NEWSPAPER)* That's right, News. Kids want to have paper routes . . .

Newspaper   They think it sounds like fun—make a little money— ride their bikes every morning . . .

Homework   But then they decide that staying in bed sounds better. Maybe it's cold . . . or maybe there's an annoying dog named Muffin who chases them every day.

Newspaper   And before long—I'm forgotten, crammed down into the bottom of a bag. Not thrown into a single yard.

Homework   Even though it's their . . . responsibility.

Newspaper   And what about my friend Homework, here? Teachers assign a paper, or something to read . . .

Homework   Right, News. The kids write it down—and sometimes they do the homework, study the spelling words,

Character Education Book of Plays
Elementary Level

write the report. But sometimes . . . they don't. They get home, play with their friends, watch a little TV—and no homework gets finished. Is it my responsibility to jump up and make a noise? I don't think so. But I don't get finished, and I don't get turned in! It's just not fair!

Newspaper *(to imaginary camera)* You can help. By giving your kids a gentle reminder . . .

Homework Like a shoe in the seat of their pants . . .

Newspaper *(a bit scolding)* Homework . . .

Homework I meant to say . . . like a note in their lunch box, or a friendly "Got any homework?" when they get home . . .

Newspaper Or maybe you could help them get up in the morning to throw their paper routes. Maybe have a little hot breakfast ready for them . . .

Homework Then maybe children everywhere will be more responsible.

Newspaper If you'd like to receive some free information . . .

Homework And a big shoe to plant in the seat . . .

Newspaper Homework . . .

Homework I meant to say . . . a free brochure . . .

Newspaper Just call 1-800-HELPAKID

Homework That's one too many numbers.

Newspaper Oh. How about 1-800-PAPERROUTE?

Homework Still too many.

Newspaper We'll work this out and get back to you.

Talk About Responsibility!

Homework   In the meantime . . . remember . . . if kids are taught responsibility . . .

Newspaper   Then people can read their newspapers.

Homework   Thank you.

Newspaper   How about 1-800-DOYOURWORK?

Homework   Still too long! Do the math!

(They exit, ad-libbing other phone numbers.)

(STAGE MANAGER enters, telling KAY)

Stage Manager   And we're live in five, four, three *(holds up two fingers, then one finger, then turns to the audience and begins clapping, urging them to do the same. AUDIENCE claps.)*

Kay   Thank you so much, ladies and gentlemen, and welcome back. We're chatting with pets whose owners aren't doing the right thing. Let's bring out our next guest. He doesn't get out much, at least not without his mobile home. He's very shy, so let's greet him quietly . . . a soft round of applause for Herman, the Hermit Crab!

(AUDIENCE applauds quietly as HERMAN enters. He looks out shyly.)

Kay   Hello, Herman the Hermit Crab, and welcome to the Kay Nine Show.

Herman   *(Taking his seat)* Thank you, Kay. It's nice of you to have me. I'm . . . I'm a little nervous in front of all of these people—I usually just stay inside my house. Or . . . er . . . shell.

Kay   And that's the point, isn't it, Herman? Your shell?

Herman   Yes. I'm having a little trouble.

Character Education Book of Plays
Elementary Level

Talk About Responsibility!

Kay   Can you explain your problem to the audience?

Herman   I'll try. *(Clears his throat, obviously not comfortable in front of a crowd.)* The girl who takes care of me does a really good job. I've been listening to some of the others *(MAMA CAT and GLUBBY look at their owners accusingly.)* and I have to say that my girl does a lot better than these two. She gives me vegetables to eat and fresh water, but there's one thing she's not taking care of for me.

Kay   And what is that, Herman?

Herman   Well, Kay, I live in empty shells. But I don't stop growing. So, every now and then I need to move up to a larger shell—until I outgrow it! But I don't guess my girl knows this, because . . . look! *(HERMAN turns around and shows his back, where there is a little tiny shell attached to his costume.)* I outgrew this shell long ago and I really need a new one!

Kay   Yes, I think it's time for an upgrade. Well, let's see what we can do! Pandra—come on out!

(PANDRA enters, very upset. She takes her seat next to HERMAN.)

Pandra   What is it, Kay? What did I do? Did I wait too long to clean him? Did his water get gross? What?

Herman   Oh, now I feel terrible. I shouldn't have come on the show!

Pandra   Oh, no, sweetie! I want to know! Whatever it is, I'll do better, I promise! What do you need?

Herman   A new shell. To live in.

Pandra   A new shell? You mean bigger?

Herman   Yes. That's all I need. Really.

Talk About Responsibility!

Pandra Well, then, good-bye, Ms. Nine. I've got to go to the beach and find Herman another shell. After all—he's my responsibility and I've got to take care of him! *(As she exits.)* Now let me see—if I catch a flight to Miami I can be back by tomorrow morning . . . One bigger shell, coming up!

Herman Wait, Pandra—they have them at the pet store . . .

Kay Well, that's all the time we have for today! I'm Kay Nine, saying . . . remember kids . . . only you have the "ability"— to have . . .

Cast . . . RESPONSIBILITY!

Kay Goodbye!

Gregory's Mom *(Facing audience and pointing)* Don't make me come lookin' for you!

(STAGE MANAGER re-enters and urges audience to applaud. All cast members wave good-bye to audience.)

Character Education Book of Plays
Elementary Level

Commit—To Commitment!
A Mini-Play About
Living Up to Commitments

Character Education Book of Plays
Elementary Level

Commit—To Commitment!

CAST

Debbie

Anna Lynn

Aunt Mimi

Uncle Toddy

Audrey

Commit—To Commitment!

Notes to the Teacher/Director

"I know I said I'd. . . . . . . (watch my brother
feed the dog
pick up my room
do my homework)

but I WANT to . . . . (go to the mall
watch TV
go to the movies
play outside.)

Who cares what I said—why can't I do what I want?!"

It can be very hard in today's world for young people to realize the value of having given their word. When the media bombards them constantly with instant gratification—new things they just have to have at the mall, at the toy store, at the supermarket—values such as living up to commitments can seem inconsequential compared to doing the next feel-good thing.

Here is a little five-character play to help reinforce the idea of commitment. Uncle Toddy and Aunt Mimi are staying with Debbie and Anna Lynn while the girls' parents are out of town. The girls have agreed to do certain chores while their parents are gone, and their aunt and uncle have made the commitment to take care of the girls. But when their friend Audrey comes over with a camping trip invitation, Debbie and Anna Lynn are ready to forget all about their agreements and take off! Uncle Toddy and Aunt Mimi, who have been arguing and picking on each other for the whole play, must make a hard decision and forbid the girls to go. But when Uncle Toddy draws a parallel between his commitment to his wife and the commitments they all have made—it becomes clear to the girls and they realize they must go camping another time.

Character Education Book of Plays
Elementary Level

Properties, Scenery, Costumes

This play is easily produced in any setting with only a table and four chairs needed for each scene. You can choose to use a large stew bowl, and smaller bowls and spoons, or simply have your cast pantomime the dishes needed for dinner. For costumes, regular clothing is fine for all three girls. The characters Uncle Toddy and Aunt Mimi can be broad and fun to portray, the perfect characters for those extroverted youngsters in your class or group. As for their appearance, they can be aged with a little baby powder in their hair. Let your actors' imaginations determine how these two look and sound. Do they wear wild Hawaiian shirts? Does Aunt Mimi wear a brightly colored muumuu and big earrings? Does Uncle Toddy wear a one-piece coverall or overalls with patches? Do they shout their lines? Talk in regional accents? Despite what your group decides about their outward appearance, the love between the older folks should be evident, even though they seem to quarrel a little.

110

Commit—To Commitment!

A Mini-Play Play About Living Up To Commitments

(As the play begins, we see a house setting, with a table and four chairs. Enter ANNA LYNN and DEBBIE, who stand center stage and speak to the audience.)

Anna Lynn   Hi, my name is Anna Lynn.

Debbie   And I'm Debbie. We're sisters. See how much we look alike?

Anna Lynn   Anyway, we're here to tell you a story about a time when we really wanted to do something—and we didn't get to do it.

Debbie   Right. It all started . . .

Anna Lynn   See, our parents . . .

Debbie   Last week . . . Anna Lynn! We sound like Aunt Mimi and Uncle Toddy!

Anna Lynn   Oh, no! We do! We're interrupting each other!

Debbie   Let's start at the beginning.

Anna Lynn   Sounds good.

(Enter AUNT MIMI, who bustles around, wiping off the table and dusting the furniture a bit.)

Debbie   That's our Aunt Mimi. She's our mother's big sister.

Anna Lynn   Our parents own a little drycleaning store in our town, and once a year they go off to a . . . what do they call it?

Debbie   A convention.

Anna Lynn   Yeah, a convention in another town. Where a bunch of

Character Education Book of Plays
Elementary Level

people who have drycleaning stores get together and talk about how to . . . make the clothes as stinky as possible, or the latest plastic bag designs . . . or something.

Debbie And when our parents leave, they worry and fret, and write big lists of stuff we need to remember—and our Aunt Mimi and Uncle Toddy come stay with us at our house.

Aunt Mimi Toddy?! Toddy! Come in here and clean up for dinner! Don't forget to take your shoes off outside the door! I don't want footprints all over my sister's rug like this was some kind of dance studio!

Uncle Toddy *(Entering, carrying his shoes, and trying to balance, holding up one stockinged foot at a time to the peep hole.)* The very idea, looking at my feet through a peep hole!

Aunt Mimi All right, that's better. You can come in. Get cleaned up for dinner.

(UNCLE TODDY enters and pantomimes rolling up his sleeves and washing his hands while AUNT MIMI bustles around the kitchen, setting the table for dinner.)

Debbie Anna Lynn and I have things we're supposed to do while Mom and Dad are out of town. I have to water the yard.

Anna Lynn It's my job to make the beds.

Debbie We're both supposed to make sure the supper dishes are clean and put away . . . oh, and one of us has to feed Sweetie Face, our dog.

Anna Lynn He's the grumpiest dog in town. I mean, he likes me and Debbie, but he won't let anyone else pet or feed him.

Debbie That's for sure. Anyway, those are our chores, plus any homework and stuff that we would be doing anyway. Oh, and we have to keep from setting ourselves on fire, busting our heads open on the bathtub . . .

Commit—To Commitment!

Anna Lynn   And we absolutely cannot throw a party for our whole class. You know—parents!

Aunt Mimi   Debbie? Anna Lynn? Where are you two? Come to supper!

Debbie   That's our cue!

Anna Lynn   Come on! *(The girls exit and re-enter the house scene.)*

Debbie   Hey, Aunt Mimi!

Aunt Mimi   Hello, girls. I've made stew for supper. Do you like stew? I don't remember.

Debbie   Sure, we like it all right.

Aunt Mimi   Great! Here you go! *(Serves bowls of stew)* So, girls, have you done your chores so far today?

Anna Lynn   Yes, Aunt Mimi. I've made all the beds . . .

Debbie   And I started the water sprinkler when I was outside earlier. I'll turn it off in about an hour.

Aunt Mimi   Well, how about the supper dishes? Have you washed those and put them away yet?

Debbie   No, Aunt Mimi . . . not yet . . .

Aunt Mimi   Why on earth not? You told your mother, my sister, that you would do these things! You made a commitment! What will I say to her . . .

Uncle Toddy   Mimi, we're just now having supper! How can they have done the dishes if we're just now using them?

Aunt Mimi   Well . . . I suppose you're right. But don't forget!

Anna Lynn   We won't. We promise.

Uncle Toddy   Mimi, leave the girls alone. Let's talk about plans for the weekend. I think I might just . . .

Character Education Book of Plays
Elementary Level

Commit—To Commitment!

(He is interrupted by a knock at the door, followed by:)

Audrey   Yoo hoo! Is anybody at home?!

Audrey   *(Entering)* Hello, everybody! Oh—sorry! I didn't know you were eating. But since you are . . . *(She gets her own bowl and helps herself to some stew. She doesn't bother to sit down; she just leans and eats.)* I've come to invite Anna Lynn and Debbie . . .

Anna Lynn   Your two best friends in all the world . . .

Audrey   Yes, of course! I want to invite my two best buddies to go camping with my family and me this weekend! It's going to be so-o-o great! We've got a cool new tent and I've got a new sleeping bag that's so-o-o soft I've been sleeping in it at home instead of my real bed. What do you say? Can you go?

Debbie   That sounds great, Audrey! Can we Aunt Mimi?

Anna Lynn   Oh please, Uncle Toddy! We haven't been camping in years!

Aunt Mimi   I don't know, girls . . . your parents left you with us, not Audrey's family . . .

Debbie   We could call Mom and Dad! We have their hotel phone number!

Uncle Toddy   Hey, hold up! What about your chores? I don't mind turning the sprinkler on and off, but you will not see me within ten feet of that growling, snapping Tyrannosaurus you girls call a dog!

Aunt Mimi   Oh, girls, your uncle's right—Sweetie Face won't eat from either one of us . . .

Uncle Toddy   No, but he might EAT one of us!

Aunt Mimi   You know what I think? We're going to have to talk about this a little bit alone. Audrey?

Audrey   Sure, go ahead!

Commit—To Commitment!

Aunt Mimi	No, I mean . . . we would like a little privacy . . .
Audrey	I closed the door when I came in—no one can hear a word you say.
Uncle Toddy	Audrey—what things tumble off the trees in autumn?
Audrey	Leaves?
Uncle Toddy	Yes. And that is what we would like for you to do.
Audrey	Oh! You'd like to talk this over without me here! I get it! I can take a hint! *(putting down her bowl.)* Thanks for the stew! *(to ANNA LYNN and DEBBIE)* Call me later and tell me what they say! Oh, I hope you can go! It's gonna be so-o-o cool! *(She exits.)*

(AUNT MIMI and UNCLE TODDY eat their stew. As though they were watching a tennis match, ANNA LYNN and DEBBIE look from AUNT MIMI . . . to UNCLE TODDY . . . to AUNT MIMI . . . back to UNCLE TODDY . . .)

Uncle Toddy	*(Finally noticing the girls)* Can't a man eat some stew in peace?
Anna Lynn	Oh, please, let us go, Uncle Toddy! Please? We'll do everything before we leave!
Aunt Mimi	Girls, it makes me sad to say 'no' to you, but I really don't think it's a good idea. I told your mother and father we would watch over you this weekend. You told them you'd do certain chores.
Uncle Toddy	And I don't want to be Sweetie Face's Happy Meal!
Aunt Mimi	If something happened to you on this camping trip, I'd never forgive myself. And your parents would never forgive me either. Oops, I almost forgot! I didn't get the mail this afternoon. You finish up your dinner and I'll be right back. *(She exits.)*
Debbie	Uncle Toddy—you really won't let us go camping with Audrey?

Commit—To Commitment!

Uncle Toddy   Girls—let me explain something to you. Your Aunt Mimi is a goofy old bird sometimes. But you know what else? She is my wife. When we got married, I promised to love and honor her. I promised to stay with her in sickness and in health, no matter how much she aggravated me about my muddy shoes. The truth is—I love the old girl. I made a commitment to her. I said I would stay with her and take care of her—and I certainly will. In the same way, she and I made a commitment to your parents—that we would watch after you this weekend. You two girls made commitments to your parents as well. So as much fun as it would be to go running off with Audrey—you really can't do that, can you?

Anna Lynn   When you put it like that . . .

Debbie   Sure would be fun, though!

Uncle Toddy   Nobody ever said keeping commitments was easy!

Aunt Mimi   *(Re-entering, carrying a sales circular)* Looky here! There's a sale on Crispy Crackle Cereal at Jumbo Foods!

Uncle Toddy   *(Looking fondly at his wife)* But some commitments are easier to keep than others.

Aunt Mimi   What are you going on about?

Uncle Toddy   Nothing! Now do you want some help cleaning off the table?

Debbie   *(To the audience.)* I know what you're thinking! How rotten! What a mean aunt and uncle!

Anna Lynn   That's what I thought at first, too. But deep down I knew they were right—when you tell somebody you'll do something —

Debbie   And they're counting on you . . .

Anna Lynn   That really is more important than doing something that seems really great at the moment.

Commit—To Commitment!

Debbie Besides, you know what? Audrey went on a hike along the creek at their camp site and got covered in poison ivy!

Anna Lynn *(Stifling a laugh)* Well, we don't mean it was a good thing . . .

Debbie Oh, no! I'm sorry she had to wear pink lotion all the rest of the weekend —

Anna Lynn But I can't say I was sorry I missed out on poison ivy!

Debbie And I'm pretty sure Sweetie Face really would have eaten Uncle Toddy.

(From offstage, a giant roar is heard.)

Anna Lynn Oh, oh! We're late with Sweetie Face's supper!

Debbie This could be dangerous! Gotta go!

Anna Lynn Bye! *(Starts to run, stops and says:)* And don't forget . . .

Debbie To live up to your commitments!

BOTH *(As they exit)* Good-bye!

The Bravest Show on Earth

A Play About Courage

Character Education Book of Plays
Elementary Level

The Bravest Show on Earth

CAST

Ringmaster

Circus Performers
  including:
  Freddy
  Danny
  Perry
  Debbie
  Nick
  Andrew
  Teresa
  Rosie

Mrs. Durand, *Rosie's Teacher*

Mom, *Rosie's mother*

Heidi

Toby

Jeanette

Caroline

Carl

Lilly Cheyenne

Billy McMeany

Tad Little

Character Education Book of Plays
Elementary Level

The Bravest Show on Earth

Notes to the Teacher/Director

Welcome to *The Bravest Show on Earth*, where participants and audience members will see three vignettes, or brief plays, regarding courage and how it can be demonstrated by young people in everyday life.

What is courage, anyway? Is it putting yourself at risk, like the acrobats in the circus? Does it necessarily involve superhuman acts of bravery? In Incentive Publication's *Character Education, Year 2, K-6*, John Heidel and Marion Lyman-Mersereau define courage as: "Firmness of mind and will in danger or difficulty." Basically, doing what you have to do, even if it is scary. Today's young people deal with different kinds of danger and difficulty regularly.

The play begins with a Ringmaster welcoming the audience and introducing the play. He or she then welcomes the Circus Performers, made up of the rest of the cast, who parade around the classroom, auditorium, cafeteria, or other performance space, playing musical instruments, holding bunches of balloons, turning cartwheels or performing other gymnastic feats, etc. After several of the cast members give testimony as to brave acts they have personally accomplished, the group divides in half and takes a seat on the stage floor, freeing up the middle of the acting area, or Center Ring, where the three vignettes will be presented. The actors in the vignettes will be part of the group of Circus Performers—they will just remove their feathers or spangles and take the stage. Following their scene, they will return to the ranks of circus performers, almost like a traveling band of actors in days of old.

The first part of the play involves the plight of Rosie, who is very frightened of giving speeches to her class. When she is assigned a speech, she tries everything she can think of to escape her fate. Finally, when she realizes that the class is really made up of just the same boys and girls with whom she eats lunch and talks every day, she overcomes her nervousness and gives a good speech.

In the second part, we see Toby and Jeanette walking to their first day at a new school in their new neighborhood. They are apprehensive about their new situation— will the work be hard? Will the kids be nice? Will the teachers be fair? There is no way to know until they make new friends, join some clubs and teams, and start to take part in their new school. The Ringmaster says, "Jeanette and Toby were scared about going to a new school, but they did what they needed to do. Even though they were scared at first, they were very courageous and brave."

The last vignette involves a bully, Billy McMeany, who steals lunch money every day from timid Lilly Cheyenne. Lilly puts up with his mistreatment until the day he

Character Education Book of Plays
Elementary Level

turns on her friend, Tad Little, who is equally shy. Lilly stands up to Billy; she defends her friend Tad. She demonstrates not only bravery, but loyalty to a friend in need of her help. The play ends with the whole cast singing a tune straight from the Big Top about bravery and courage in everyday life.

This play is written for a large cast, but the script has flexibility. If your group is smaller, actors featured as Circus Performers with one line at the beginning and a line in the song could easily play roles in a vignette. On the other hand, you may include additional actors as Circus Performers—they may march in the parade at the beginning, help with set changes, and sing in the closing song. You may also wish to have your class think of additional one-line testimonials for the beginning of the play, and include as many as time allows.

Your scenic and prop needs are minimal, and costuming consists mostly of normal school clothes, with the exception of the circus attire at the beginning, which can be authentic or created out of construction paper.

Words that may be new to your cast include:

feats

reluctantly

astound

fumbling

miserable

timidly

cringing

completely

A worksheet is included to help familiarize your cast with these words.

So get popcorn, peanuts, and cotton candy in hand, and join us for *The Bravest Show on Earth.*

The Bravest Show on Earth

Properties

- A thermometer
- Sunglasses
- Hat
- Notecards
- Backpacks for Toby, Jeanette, Caroline, and Carl
- Art supplies, including crayons and paper
- Money for Billy to take from Lilly (can be pantomimed)
- A dollar

Scenery

The most important scenic challenge of this play is to somehow designate the Center Ring. Suggestions include:

- securing corrugated bulletin board border to the floor to create a ring that stands up a few inches;
- putting down coffee cans filled with sand or something else heavy, and winding crepe paper streamers around them two or three inches off the floor;
- using colored tape to mark a big circle in the center of the floor.

You will need to designate the spot for the testimonials to take place early in the play. A microphone would be good if one is available. If a microphone is not available, just have the actors speak from center stage—or have a small platform or crate which could be painted in circus colors on which your actors could stand.

A classroom desk is needed for Rosie's scene.

Character Education Book of Plays
Elementary Level

Costumes

Ringmaster needs a black top hat, which can be found at a costume rental or party supply store, or created out of black construction paper with a cardboard bill. He should have a black coat (a thrift store item), which would be even more authentic with tails! Could Mom or Dad sew black fabric onto the bottom of a black jacket to create the look of tails?

The circus performers can be as officially (or as creatively!) costumed as you like. Costume rental stores certainly have all the lion tamer, acrobat, and tight-rope walker costumes you could want, but it might be more fun to have all performers dress, for instance, in solid black and then add costume pieces. Gather netting to form a lovely boa, for instance, or create a head piece by gluing craft store feathers to a construction paper head band. (They might wish to carry stuffed animals to represent lions and tigers to be tamed.) This approach would work especially well if some of your actors were playing more than one part; have the actor drop off the acrobat's sequined jacket and put on a school backpack.

The actors playing Rosie's Mom and Mrs. Durand may wish to add a jacket or a pair of glasses or earrings to create an older look. (If these actors are not playing other parts, you may wish to add just a bit of baby powder to their temples.)

The rest of the cast should wear regular school clothes. Make sure that Rosie has pockets for her hat and sunglasses, and that Lilly Cheyenne and Tad Little also have pockets for their money.

The Bravest Show on Earth

Teaching Materials to Accompany *The Bravest Show on Earth*

Class Discussion

When Rosie is trying to avoid giving her speech, her mother does not believe that Rosie is actually sick. She tries to discover the reason that Rosie might be trying to avoid school. Similarly, Rosie's teacher, Mrs. Durand, pushes Rosie to go ahead and get started with her research, even though she knows Rosie is trying to avoid giving the speech. As a class, discuss whether these two adults are "being mean" to Rosie, or helping her. Should Rosie's Mom write a fake note and let her stay home sick? How would this help or hurt Rosie? Should Mrs. Durand give Rosie an alternate assignment? What sort of lesson would this teach Rosie, and would it be a valuable one to learn?

Writing Exercise

1. Have your class write brief papers regarding something they have done which was scary. Urge them to focus on activities which were for their own good, or for the good of someone else. Maybe they had to help with a tough decision about putting a very ill pet to sleep, or had to play a musical instrument in a recital situation. You might consider choosing the most interesting (or humorous) two or three and include them in the testimonials at the beginning of the play.

2. Have the girls in your class write a diary entry as though they were Rosie. Change things slightly—have them pretend that she WAS allowed to chicken out of giving her speech about Mars. Now it is that evening, and she is writing in her diary. How would she feel? What might she write?

3. In an exercise similar to #2, have the boys in your class assume the role of Toby and write a letter to a friend back home. In the letter, let Toby tell how he froze up completely on his way to his first day of school, and turned around and ran back home. How might he feel if this had been the way he handled his fear? What would he tell his buddy back home?

Art Projects

Have a circus art day! See Costumes for ideas about items which could be created by your artistic class. You might consider creating banners and other decorations for your acting space. If the public is invited to your performance, make colorful, circus-themed posters to put around the school and in local businesses. Your class might wish to make brightly-colored programs or tickets to hand out in advance and collect at the door the day of the performance.

Character Education Book of Plays
Elementary Level

Vocabulary Worksheet

The Bravest Show on Earth

1. Which of the following sentences most correctly uses the word **feat**?
   a. _____ My feat hurt, so I took off my shoes.
   b. _____ Bringing up his math grade was quite a feat!
   c. _____ We saw many feats in the art gallery.

2. If you **astound** someone, what do you do to them?
   a. _____ Shock or surprise them
   b. _____ Hurt them
   c. _____ Put a blindfold on them

3. Which of these things is most likely to make you feel **miserable**?
   a. _____ Swimming
   b. _____ Chicken pox
   c. _____ Opening birthday presents

4. If a person is **cringing**, are they:
   a. _____ Singing loudly
   b. _____ Grilling hamburgers or steaks in the back yard
   c. _____ Shrinking back, as though afraid

5. Which of these things would you most likely do **reluctantly**?
   a. _____ Eat a piece of chocolate
   b. _____ Pack up your towel and other things on the last day of a beach visit
   c. _____ Go bike riding with a friend

6. Which of these is the most correct use of the word **fumbling**?
   a. _____ She was fumbling her math homework very carefully to make sure it was correct.
   b. _____ He knew he should've gotten a shopping cart; he was fumbling the eggs!
   c. _____ Fumbling is the secret of our lovely green yard.

7. Kim answered the teacher **timidly** when she was called upon in class. Did she:
   a. _____ Speak softly and shyly
   b. _____ Get up on her desk and shout out the answer
   c. _____ Run into the hall and sing the answer as if she were an opera star

8. If someone does something **completely**, they do it:
   a. _____ Almost all the way
   b. _____ Really badly
   c. _____ Totally

The Bravest Show on Earth

A Play About Courage

(This play takes place in a circus setting. There is a Center Ring in which courage-related scenes will take place, and an area around the Center Ring in which a parade takes place. As the play begins, RINGMASTER enters and addresses the audience.)

Ringmaster Hello, ladies and gentlemen, boys and girls, and welcome to the Bravest Show On Earth! Prepare to be amazed, because today you will see feats of bravery beyond your wildest imagination! You will see displays of courage that will amaze and astound you! Today's circus will be a little different than the ones you are probably used to. When you think of courage and brave acts, maybe you think of lion tamers forcing the mighty lion away with a whip and a chair. Maybe you picture daring young men and women on the flying trapeze, or acrobats walking on tiny tightropes. These performers are all very brave, but there are many other ways of showing courage, and many people do so every day! What is courage anyway? Really, it's keeping your head and doing what needs to be done in the face of danger or difficulty! That doesn't always mean putting your head in the lion's mouth.

(CIRCUS PERFORMERS start to enter and parade around.)

Don't take my word for it! Listen as our brave circus performers tell you stories of their own special brands of courage!

(The CIRCUS PERFORMERS march in excitedly, juggling balls, waving flags, and playing musical instruments. The CIRCUS PERFORMERS continue to march around the room, but when each of the following people reach the designated spot, he or she proudly describes to the audience his or her brave act.)

Freddy I rolled up my sleeve and got a shot and I didn't cry!

Danny I told the truth about the kid who tossed the baseball through my dad's new car—it was me!

*Character Education Book of Plays
Elementary Level*

Debbie   I took my achievement test! *(Insert the name of the current much-feared achievement-type test being administered in schools in your area.)*

Perry   I faced a whole room full of aunts and uncles! Yuck! Kisses for days!

Nick   I went to the dentist!

Andrew   I played football against a team from another school.

Teresa   *(To Andrew)* What's so brave about that?

Andrew   They were all twice as big as me! Roar!

(He "roars," striking a menacing football pose)

Ringmaster   *(Taking back over, as the CIRCUS PERFORMERS divide and sit on either side of the Center Ring.)* As you can see, little things can be brave things! Turn your attention now please to the Center Ring.

(Enter ROSIE, who enters the Center Ring and faces the audience.)

This is Rosie.

(ROSIE waves at the audience.)

Rosie   Hello. It's me, Rosie the Coward.

Ringmaster   Rosie, you're not a coward! You were brave . . . you stood right up . . . oh, wait, I'm getting ahead of myself. Rosie had an assignment for school.

Rosie   I had to give a speech!

Ringmaster   She had to give a speech!

Rosie   About something that I found interesting! You know what I found interesting? Not giving speeches!

Ringmaster   Rosie is interested in the planet Mars.

Rosie   *(Sighing)* It's true.

The Bravest Show on Earth

Ringmaster   Rosie . . . won't you show us what happened?

(RINGMASTER exits, or takes his seat with the other CIRCUS PERFORMERS)

Rosie   Oh yes, I suppose. See, it all started one day in school . . .

(A circus performer sets up a school desk for Rosie, in which she sits. Enter MRS. DURAND, Rosie's teacher.)

Mrs. Durand   Good morning class, and welcome back from the weekend. I'm very excited to give you your six-week project assignments today.

Rosie   *(Under her breath, but loudly enough for the audience to hear)* Oh please, not a speech, oh please, oh please . . .

Mrs. Durand   I thought about having you all create something for me out of clay . . .

Rosie   Clay is good . . . I like clay . . .

Mrs. Durand   But your art teacher tells me you'll be working with clay in art class this week. So I thought about a photography project, where you could all take pictures of interesting things and bring them into class.

Rosie   I love to take pictures! Cameras are my life!

Mrs. Durand   Then I realized that you may not all have a camera and that wouldn't be fair. So I came up with the best idea of all!

Rosie   Oh please no, not a speech . . .

Mrs. Durand   You will all make . . .

Rosie   Pot holders?

Mrs. Durand   Speeches! You will all make speeches on something that interests you. They don't need to be very long . . . just two or three minutes will be fine . . . but make sure you know your topic well! Make them interesting! Delight your audience!

Character Education Book of Plays
Elementary Level

The Bravest Show on Earth

Rosie   Try not to lose your lunch all over their shoes . . .

Mrs. Durand   Now, you may all go to the library and begin researching your topic!

Rosie   *(Rising from her chair, which a CIRCUS PERFORMER whisks away.)* Mrs. Durand? May I speak to you a minute?

Mrs. Durand   Yes, Rosie, what can I do for you?

Rosie   You can excuse me from this assignment.

Mrs. Durand   Why, Rosie, why on earth would I do that? I know you will write a speech about Mars, which you love, and I look forward to learning all about it!

Rosie   But I hate to speak in public! It makes me nervous! I have clammy hands just thinking about it! My tongue is dry! I feel dizzy!

Mrs. Durand   Well, you may be coming down with the flu, but you're not excused from this speech. Now get down to the library and start writing!

(MRS. DURAND exits. ROSIE faces the audience.)

Rosie   I can't explain why I was so scared of speaking. I mean, it was just my class—gross old Timmy Green who wiped his nose on his jacket sleeve, and Jim Doolin who brought banana and onion sandwiches in his lunch every day—I mean, they weren't anyone scary! So what was it about standing up and giving a speech? I didn't know—and I still don't—but I know I tried everything to get out of it. *(Enter MOM with a thermometer.)* Mom! I'm so glad you're here. I feel awful! I'm sure I have a temperature!

Mom   Really? *(Feels ROSIE'S head.)* You don't feel warm . . . well, let's see. Lift up your tongue. *(Places thermometer under ROSIE'S tongue and looks at her watch.)* Hmmm. What kind of disease can this be? Is it a "gotta run the

The Bravest Show on Earth

mile in PE" disease? No, your class has already run the mile. Is it a "gross boy moved behind me in class" disease? *(ROSIE shakes her head 'no.')* Not that, huh? What else could it be . . . wait! I've got it! It's a "Sloppy Joe for lunch in the cafeteria" disease! Don't worry, honey, I'll pack you a lunch!

Rosie *(Trying to talk around the thermometer)* Why, no, Mom, it's not any of these! I'm . . .

(MOM takes out the thermometer)

I'm really sick. And if you let me stay home, I won't miss much, really! We're not doing anything in Math, I've already turned in my report in Social Studies, and in English we just have these speeches . . . *(ROSIE realizes what she has said and claps her hand over her mouth)*

Mom Ah ha, that's it. The dreaded SPEECH DAY. Nice try, Princess, but you're going to school and giving a speech about Mars. I heard you practicing in your room last night! It sounded great.

Rosie But, Mom!

Mom *(Putting her arm around ROSIE.)* I don't know why you're so worried. You'll do fine! You're funny, you're smart, you're cute . . . and you won't throw up on anyone's shoes, no matter what you think. Now go finish getting ready and make your speech! You'll be great!

(MOM exits.)

Rosie Thanks a lot Mom. Anyway, I went on to school, and found my best friend Heidi.

(Enter HEIDI)

Heidi Hi, Rosie.

Rosie Hi'dy, Heidi. I'm so miserable—I have to give my speech today.

Character Education Book of Plays Elementary Level

Heidi   Oh, you'll do fine, Rosie. I'm giving my speech tomorrow—here's what it's called: "Hair Gel—Miracle Product or Sticky Goo?"

Rosie   Gee, Heidi, that sounds deep.

Heidi   Yeah. I can't wait.

Rosie   Hey, Heidi, I have a great idea! Why don't you put on my sunglasses *(pulls sunglasses out of pocket)* and my hat *(pulls a hat out also)* and pretend to be me and give my speech for me! It's all written out on notecards!

Heidi   Rosie, you are crazy? Nobody would ever believe I was you! We look nothing alike!

Rosie   I know, I know. It was worth a try.

Heidi   I think it was worth a nickel. Bye, Rosie! I'll see you in class!

Rosie   *(To audience)* I know, "it was worth a nickel" didn't make any sense. But that's Heidi. Anyway, I had one more plan up my sleeve . . .

(CIRCUS PERFORMER enters and re-sets classroom desk. ROSIE sits in it, and MRS. DURAND enters)

Mrs. Durand   All right, let's get started with our speeches. Who wants to go first? I know . . . Rosie!

(ROSIE points to her throat, out of which no sound is coming)

What is it, Rosie? You've lost your voice? You can't talk? Not even a little bit?

(ROSIE nods in answer to the first two questions, shakes her head "no" to the last one)

That is so tragic! *(Points away)* Why, look there! It's _____ ! *(Insert the name of a "heart-throb" teen actor, singer or group)*

Rosie   What? Where!

The Bravest Show on Earth

Mrs. Durand She has her voice back! What a miracle! Now, let's hear a speech about Mars, Miss Rosie! *(Exits, sitting down with CIRCUS PERFORMERS)*

Rosie *(Reluctantly rising and fumbling notecards out of her pockets)* Well . . . let's see . . . my speech today is about Mars . . . Mars is often called the Red Planet, because the soil is red . . . *(To audience)* I was so nervous I could hardly breathe. No kidding. My knees were jumping around like they were on a trampoline, and I felt all hot and sweaty—but then the weirdest thing happened. I looked out at my class and realized that they were all just kids. Just . . . my class. They didn't care if I said everything exactly right or not—they were just waiting for their turn, and either dreading it, like me, or looking forward to talking about hair gel, like Heidi. So I stopped being so silly and just . . . talked about Mars. And I did fine . . . and I got an "A."

Ringmaster *(Re-entering and joining HEIDI in the Center Ring.)* Did you go running from the classroom?

Rosie Nope. I did my speech.

Ringmaster Did anything bad happen to you?

Rosie Not a thing.

Ringmaster You were scared—but you gave your speech anyway. Ladies and gentlemen—I give you—COURAGE!

(RINGMASTER leads the audience in applauding. CIRCUS PERFORMERS strike the chair. ROSIE bows and says:)

Rosie And I didn't barf on anyone's shoes!

(She takes her place with the CIRCUS PERFORMERS.)

Ringmaster Next up, here are some other brave kids—Toby and Jeanette Summers!

(Enter TOBY and JEANETTE, carrying backpacks and arguing.)

The Bravest Show on Earth

Toby I tell you, spaghetti is better than pizza! It just is, that's all! It just IS!

Jeanette You are SO not right. Pizza is so much better! Spaghetti is just . . . just . . . noodles! Shaped like worms! Worms with sauce!

Toby Girls! I'll never understand you as long as I live! I suppose you think volleyball is a better sport than baseball!

Ringmaster You'd never guess that they are brother and sister, would you? Jeanette and Toby have just moved to a completely new city . . . in a completely new state . . . and today is the first day of a completely new school. As they walk to this new school, a thousand questions are in their minds. What will it be like? Will the kids be nice? Will the work be hard? It takes courage to face these questions and a whole new world. So they are arguing about things that do not matter, like spaghetti and pizza—to keep from talking about the things that are really scaring them.

Jeanette Look, Toby, we're almost there.

Toby I miss my friends back home.

Jeanette Me too.

Toby Oh, no, here come two kids. They're probably going to try to beat us up and steal our lunch money! Or make fun of us!

Jeanette Should we run?

(Enter CAROLINE and CARL. They are also carrying backpacks and headed for school.)

Caroline Hi.

Jeanette Hi.

Carl Do you guys live around here?

The Bravest Show on Earth

Toby   Yeah, we just moved in this summer. We're going to _____ *(Insert the name of your school here.)*

Caroline   That's where we go. It's pretty cool.

Jeanette   Really?

Caroline   Yeah. We have lots of fun clubs and stuff to do after school. There's a United Nations Club and a Stock Market Club—oh, and the best one of all—an After School Drama Club! We play theatre games and stuff—it's great.

Toby   I played baseball back home. Is there a team here?

Carl   Are you kidding? I play for the Tigers. *(Or insert school team if you have one.)* We won for our district last year!

Toby   All right! Maybe I can try out for the team!

Jeanette   He's a pretty good catcher even if he is my brother.

Caroline   Aren't little brothers the worst? Carl is mine. Oh, my name's Caroline. What's yours?

Jeanette   I'm Jeanette. And this is Toby.

Carl   My name is Carl. Come on, Toby. I'll race you to the gym!

Toby   You're on! *(The boys exit, racing.)*

Caroline   What makes them so weird? Racing to school on the first day!

Jeanette   I have no idea. So, tell me more about this After School Drama Club. Do you put on plays?

(The girls exit, ad-libbing about the clubs at school and other girl topics, and RINGMASTER re-enters.)

Ringmaster   Looks like Toby and Jeanette have two new friends already. And that's good, because at lunch later, they tripped on a backpack and spilled meatloaf all over the cafeteria!

Character Education Book of Plays
Elementary Level

The Bravest Show on Earth

(JEANETTE and TOBY have joined the other CIRCUS PERFORMERS. At this line, they jump up and say:)

Jeanette   We did not.

Toby   That didn't happen!

Ringmaster   I was just kidding.

(JEANETTE and TOBY sit back down.)

Jeanette and Toby were scared about going to a new school, but they did what they needed to do—met some new friends, started taking part in clubs and teams—and before long, they felt right at home. Even though they were scared at first, they were very COURAGEOUS and BRAVE . . . especially when that meatloaf went flying! Let's hear it for them!

(RINGMASTER leads the audience in applauding while JEANETTE and TOBY shake their fists.)

Ringmaster   Last but not least, please welcome to the Center Ring Lilly Cheyenne and Bully McMeany!

(Enter LILLY CHEYENNE and BILLY McMEANY.)

Billy McMeany   Hey! My name's Billy, not Bully.

Ringmaster   Sorry, my mistake. These two classmates were in the same art class at school . . .

(Enter CIRCUS PERFORMERS with two desks, and crayons and paper. LILLY CHEYENNE and BILLY McMEANY sit in the desks.)

Every day, Billy pestered Lilly.

Billy McMeany   Hey Lilly. Let me borrow your crayons. I left mine at home.

Lilly Cheyenne   *(Timidly)* Billy, you borrow my crayons every day. Can't you remember to bring your own?

The Bravest Show on Earth

Billy McMeany *(Leaning over toward LILLY and making a mean face at her.)* I wasn't asking, I was telling! Hand over your crayons! NOW!

Lilly Cheyenne *(Cringing)* Oh, all right, Billy. Here. *(Gives BILLY McMEANY her crayons)*

Billy McMeany Oh, and I need some lunch money, too!

Lilly Cheyenne But, Billy! If I give you my lunch money, I won't have any!

Billy McMeany Well, wah wah wah, little cry baby! I guess you need to start bringing a little bit more money, huh?

Lilly Cheyenne *(Handing over her lunch money)* Billy, why are you so mean?

Billy McMeany Me? Mean? Why are you such a wimp? See ya around, Lilly—I've got to go have some lunch. *(Looks at the money in his hand)* I guess I can't get too much for this little bit of change. Do better tomorrow, Lilly, or . . . or else! *(He shakes a fist in LILLY'S frightened face, then exits. CIRCUS PERFORMERS strike chairs and art supplies.)*

Lilly Cheyenne *(To audience)* I don't know why I let him push me around like that! I guess it was partly because I was scared of him—I didn't really think he would hurt me, but I couldn't be sure. But also I think I wanted everyone to like me . . . I just couldn't say no! But one day . . .

(TAD LITTLE enters and faces the audience.)

This is my friend, Tad Little.

Tad Little How 'ya doin'?

Lilly Cheyenne Tad and I had been friends since . . .

Tad Little Since we were two and in a play group. I finger-painted your hair—you glued my shirt to my mother's purse. We've been pals ever since.

Character Education Book of Plays
Elementary Level

The Bravest Show on Earth

Lilly Cheyenne   The other day, Tad and I were on the playground . . .

Tad Little   When up came Bully McMeany.

Billy McMeany   *(Entering)* Hey! My name is Billy, not Bully!

Tad Little   Sorry, my mistake.

Lilly Cheyenne   Anyway, we were just talking, not bothering anybody . . .

Billy McMeany   Hey! I need some money for the ice cream truck after school.

Lilly Cheyenne   I already gave you all my money, Billy, at lunch today! Remember?

Billy McMeany   Yeah, and I spent it on lunch! Now I need some more! If I don't get a root beer-flavored frozen pop, I don't know what might happen. Hey . . . how about you, you little creep? *(He moves toward TAD LITTLE.)* You got any money?

Tad Little   No. I don't have any. Now leave me alone.

Billy McMeany   I bet you do have some money in your pockets! Now hand it over! I need ice cream!

Tad Little   I don't have any money, I tell you!

Billy McMeany   So you don't have any money, huh? Well, let's just see . . . *(starts to stick his hands into TAD LITTLE'S pockets)*

Lilly Cheyenne   Leave him alone, Billy!

Tad Little   Yeah! Leave me alone! I don't have . . .

Billy McMeany   *(pulling a dollar out of TAD LITTLE'S pockets.)* You don't have what? This?

Tad Little   That's my dues for Boy Scouts! Give it back!

Billy McMeany   Oh, no, I don't think so! I think this is MY dues—for the

The Bravest Show on Earth

ice cream truck! Now don't you ever lie to me again, you shrimp, or I'll . . .

(LILLY CHEYENNE has heard enough. She comes between the two boys and sticks her fist right up in BILLY McMEANY'S face.)

Lilly Cheyenne   Hold it, Billy, just hold it right there! You have swiped my lunch money from me all year, but you are not going to steal from my friend Tad. I know what the problem is, Billy McMeany—you spend your money at the video arcade and are too scared to ask your parents for any more!

Billy McMeany   Why you little . . . you little . . . girl! I'll mop the floor with you!

Lilly Cheyenne   I don't think you're going to mop the floor with anybody, Billy McMeany! I think you are a big old coward and a creep and you need to leave Tad and me and everybody else in our class alone! You need to stop wasting your money in the mall or wherever you go when the rest of us are doing good things like Boy Scouts! And if you're not man enough to do that, at least be enough of a man to ask your own mother for more money instead of trying to scare it out of kids who are smaller than you!

Billy McMeany   But I . . . I . . .

Lilly Cheyenne   You . . . you what? Now get out of here, you creep! Go home and leave me and my friends alone, Bully McMeany!

Billy McMeany   My name is Billy, not Bully!

Lilly Cheyenne   Sorry, my mistake!

(BILLY McMEANY hangs his head and exits, while the RINGMASTER enters, and leads the audience in applauding and cheering. TAD LITTLE raises up LILLY'S fist as though she is a prize fighter.)

Ringmaster   Brava! Brava! Well done, Lilly! How BRAVE of you to defend your friend Tad!

Character Education Book of Plays
Elementary Level

The Bravest Show on Earth

Tad Little I guess it's a good thing I finger-painted her hair that time! What a cool friend!

Lilly Cheyenne No problem, pal! Next time, you can take on the bully—I mean Billy!

(They exit to re-join the other CIRCUS PERFORMERS.)

Ringmaster Thank you to all our performers today for showing that there are all sorts of ways to be brave. But boys and girls—if you see real danger, or someone threatens you, don't hesitate to ask for help from an adult, or run away. Don't confuse courage with putting yourself in danger. And now, in the center ring, allow me to present . . . the circus performers!

(The whole cast assembles and sings:)

Cast EVERY DAY, AT SCHOOL AND AT PLAY,
BRAVERY IS SHOWN IN A HUNDRED WAYS.
STUDY REAL HARD AND TAKE THAT TEST,
CAN'T MAKE A HUNDRED? JUST DO YOUR BEST!

Perry 'WORLD'S BRAVEST KID' SHOULD BE MY TITLE
I'M PLAYING IN A BIG RECITAL!

Rosie GOTTA MAKE A SPEECH? HEY, DON'T BE SCARED!
PICTURE THE CROWD IN ITS UNDERWEAR!

Cast OH, SOMETIMES COURAGE IS HARD TO SEE
BUT IT CAN BE SHOWN BY HIM . . . OR ME!
OH, BASES LOADED, YOUR TURN TO BAT
EVEN MARK MCGWIRE WAS A 'FRAIDY CAT!

(Music pauses)

Danny *(Speaking)* Well, maybe not Mark McGwire . . .

Cast LATE AT NIGHT, A NOISE IN THE CLOSET.
WHAT'S THAT SOUND? WHAT COULD CAUSE IT?
JUST REACH OVER, TURN ON THE LIGHT,
A KITTY IS THE MONSTER
    IN THE MIDDLE OF THE NIGHT!

The Bravest Show on Earth

Freddy *(Impersonating a cat)* Rowl!

Cast BE STRONG, BE BRAVE, BE COURAGEOUS AND TRUE
OH, EVEN THOUGH SOMETIMES IT'S HARD TO DO
OH, DON'T BE AFRAID AT YOUR NEW SCHOOL

Jeanette, Toby, Caroline & Carl OLD FRIENDS ARE GREAT, BUT NEW FRIENDS ARE COOL!

Cast STAND UP TO THOSE WHO DON'T ACT RIGHT.
THEY ARE MOSTLY BARK, AND DO NOT OFTEN BITE.
SOMETIMES BEING SCARED IS DOWNRIGHT SILLY

Lilly Cheyenne JUST SHAKE YOUR FIST AT A BULLY NAMED BILLY!

Cast OH, EVERY DAY, ALL OVER THE PLACE
OH, BRAVERY CAN SHOW ITS MIGHTY FACE
OH, KEEP YOUR HEAD
IF YOU'RE WEAK IN THE KNEES.
YOU DON'T HAVE TO SWING
FROM THE HIGH TRAPEZE!

(Spoken)

Be brave, everybody!

The Bravest Show on Earth

"Brave Every Day"

Lyrics by Judy Truesdell Mecca

Music by Jenifer Truesdell Christman

Tum tum tum tum tum tum tum tum tum tum Ev-ry day, at school and at play.

brav-er-y is shown in a hun-dred ways. Stu-dy real hard and take that test,

can't make a hun-dred? Just do your best! 'World's brav-est kid' should be my tit-le.

I'm play-ing in a big re-ci-tal! Got-ta make a speech? Hey, don't be scar-ed!

pic-ture the crowd in its un-der-wear! Oh, Some-times cour-age is hard to see. But

it can be shown by him or me! Oh, Bas-es load-ed, your turn to bat ev-en

Mark Mc-Gwire was a 'fraid-y cat. Well, Maybe not Mark McGwire... Late at night a

noise in the clo-set. What's that sound? What could cause it? Just reach o-ver

The Bravest Show on Earth

Be brave, everybody!

Character Education Book of Plays
Elementary Level